Preface

Many years ago as pastor of the Emmanuel Baptist Church, Alexandria, Louisiana, I taught a class in Bible interpretation at nearby Louisiana College. A labor of love to help relieve a shortage of teachers during World War II, it was one of the most rewarding experiences of my ministry. One day we were talking about the importance of doctrinal preaching. One student asked, "But isn't doctrinal preaching dry?" The reply, "The preacher may be dry, but doctrine never is."

At about the same time I preached in a revival meeting in Muskogee, Oklahoma, where W. A. Criswell was then pastor. The Sunday morning sermon on salvation by grace through faith was broadcast over radio. It was very much a doctrinal sermon, but presented in a positive manner. Early that afternoon I received a phone call from a woman of another denomination complimenting the sermon. She said, "The thing I liked most about it was that it had no *doctrine* in it!" She identified "doctrine" with beating people of different beliefs over the head.

The fact of the matter is that "doctrine," from the Latin *doctrina*, means "teaching." It is that which is taught or presented for acceptance or belief. In the Christian sense it embodies truth as taught by or about Jesus Christ as God's revelation (John 7:16-17). As such, *doctrine* is not the private province of preachers. It is an area belonging to all believers. It is something to be believed, practiced, and taught.

The multiplicity of inquiries from lay people as to what the Bible teaches about various matters shows their deep and widespread interest in doctrine. It was with joy, therefore, that I accepted the invitation of the publisher to write this little book. It should be stated, however, that its contents are my own expression of my understanding of the doctrines treated. It is my hope and prayer that this work will prove helpful to all who want to be "ready always to give an answer to every man that asketh you the reason of the hope that is in you" (1 Pet. 3:15).

I wish to take this opportunity to express undying love and appreciation to my wife and helpmate through the years—and now also my "retirement secretary"—whose typing skill has put my *hen-scratching* into readable form, thus making this volume and many others possible.

Herschel H. Hobbs, Pastor-Emeritus,
First Baptist Church,
Oklahoma City, Oklahoma

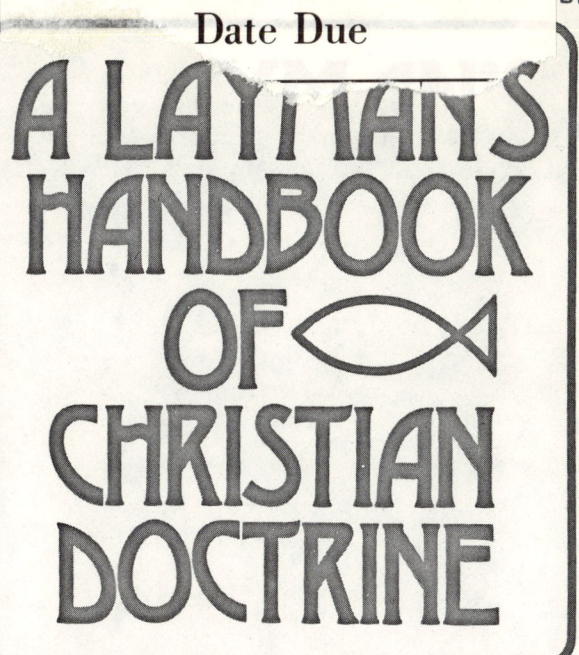

A Layman's Handbook of Christian Doctrine

HERSCHEL H. HOBBS

BROADMAN PRESS
Nashville, Tennessee

Dedication

To every person, layman or pastor, who in the spirit of the Bereans "received the word with all readiness of mind, and searched the scriptures daily, whether those things were so" (Acts 17:11).

© Copyright 1974 • Broadman Press
All rights reserved

4219-27
ISBN: 0-8054-1927-6

Library of Congress Catalog Card Number: 74-78615
Dewey Decimal Classification: 230
Printed in the United States of America

A Layman's Handbook of Christian Doctrine

Adoption. The word "adoption" is found five times in the New Testament and is used only by Paul (Rom. 8:15,23; 9:4; Gal. 4:5; Eph. 1:5). The Greek word means "a placing or making of a son." His idea is drawn from the Roman law of adoption, and corresponds to Jesus' vital figure of the new birth.

Under this law a man might adopt another man's son, or, more often, a slave. In a ceremony before five witnesses the adopting father paid the price of manumission and stood responsible for future debts. The price paid in Paul's use of this figure was the redemptive work of Christ (Gal. 4:4-5). The transaction was witnessed by the Holy Spirit (Rom. 8:16).

The adopted son was said to have been born again into a new family with new relationships. He became a joint-heir with naturally-born sons of all his father had. But he also accepted the responsibilities of sonship. Paul's spiritual application of this is seen in Romans 8:17. He received both the suffering and glory with Christ. And the glory so far outweighs the suffering that they cannot be compared (Rom. 8:18). "Reckon" was a bookkeeping term. So Paul drew a trial balance with the above discovery.

It should be noted that in Romans 8:23 "adoption" is used with respect to the resurrection or redemption (full-redemption) of the body. Thus "adoption" involves full-salvation: regeneration, sanctification, glorification (see also "full-redemption" in Eph. 1:14). See *New Birth; Salvation.*

Antichrist. See *Christ, Anti.*

Armageddon. See *Har-Magedon.*

Atonement. The idea of atonement is central in God's purpose in history. The English word "atonement" appears often in the Old Testament. But it is found only once in the New Testament (Rom. 5:11, KJV). But many other versions (cf. American Revised Version) render it here as "reconciliation." However, the idea of atonement runs throughout the New Testament.

In the Old Testament the Hebrew words so translated mean respectively "to cover" and to offer or receive a sin offering. These apply to the relationship between God and man. One word deals with effecting harmony between men (reconcile, 1 Sam. 29:4). The verb "to cover" is the one used most often. In the New Testament the Greek word most often used means "to cause to be friendly" or "to restore" in the sense of removing enmity. The idea of reconciliation pervades the meaning of atonement (2 Cor. 5:19-21). It should be noted, however, that nowhere do the Scriptures teach that God needs reconciling to man, but man to God. God always takes the initiative in providing atonement: in the Old Testament through the system of sacrifice and offering; in the New Testament supremely through Jesus Christ (2 Cor. 5:19).

Basic in the idea of atonement is the thought of a broken fellowship between God and man because of man's sin (Gen. 3; Isa. 59:1-2). God created man for fellowship with himself. And his redemptive purpose is to provide the conditions whereby man may return to that fellowship. So the word "atonement" may be seen as *at-one-ment,* that man may be at one with God in character and spiritual fellowship. A holy God cannot condone or ignore sin. So he has moved in history to cover man's sin in the blood of Christ, his very life principle. This truth is foreshadowed in the Old Testament sacrificial system which is fulfilled as the *true* sacrifice in the life and death of his Son (Heb. 7:22-27; 9:11 to 10:12).

Christ is seen as "the Lamb slain from the foundation of the world" (Rev. 13:8; also 5:9,12-13). In his omniscience (all wisdom) God knew before creating man that he would sin and become estranged from him. "The Lamb slain" speaks of the eternal nature of God's redemptive purpose (see *Redeem*). Forgiveness was in God's heart before sin was in man's heart. And his atoning work was wrought out in the arena of history through his Son, the Lamb (John 1:29; Heb. 10:4-10; Rev. 5:6,9,12-14).

The New Testament clearly centers the atonement in Jesus Christ. It involves his life, death, and resurrection. In his life the eternal Word or Christ became flesh (see *Word*) and tabernacled among men (John 1:1,14). Virgin born, he was God's Son. Born of the virgin Mary, he was the "Son of man" (Matt. 1:18-21; Luke 1:26-38). He lived in a flesh-and-blood body in a corrupt world. He was tempted in all points like as we are, yet without sin (Heb. 4:15; Matt. 4:1-11). Thus he proved God "just" (Rom. 3:26) in his demand for righteousness. Then he became *sin* for us, dying on a cross to pay the price for sin (Rom. 3:26; 6:23; 2 Cor. 5:21), that in him God might be the "justifier of him which believeth in Jesus" (Rom. 3:26). He created the condition whereby men through faith in his Son may be at-one with him. The atonement is for all men. But it becomes such in fact only for those who through God's grace receive his Son as Savior (Eph. 2:8-10).

The atonement involves the entire Godhead. God the Father proposed it; God the Son provided it; God the Holy Spirit propagates it as he effects regeneration in the believer and through such proclaims it to a lost world (John 3:6; Acts 1:8).

Atonement, Day of. The Day of Atonement was an annual occasion held on the tenth day of the seventh month (Lev. 23:27; also Exod. 30:10). This would be in the early fall (e.g., Sept. 16, 1974; Sept. 15, 1975). It was called a "holy convocation" of all the children of Israel, a day on which no work was to be done (Lev. 16:31; 23:27). In addition to the various sacrifices and offerings throughout the year, it was to provide an annual atonement for the people's sins. No one other than the high priest was allowed to enter the Holy of Holies, and that only on this day (Lev. 16:2ff.).

The details concerning the Day of Atonement are found in Leviticus 16. On this day the people assembled before the tabernacle. Certain rituals were observed and sacrifices made by Aaron, the high priest, before he entered the "holy place within the veil" (see *Veil*) or the Holy of Holies where God was said to dwell in mercy with his people.

For the sacrifices on the Day of Atonement certain animals were prescribed: a young bull, two kids of the goats, and a ram for a burnt offering, for the high priest and the people (vv. 3,5,24).

First, Aaron washed himself and put on holy linen garments (v. 4). Then he sacrificed the bullock for his sins and those of his family (v. 11). This was done in the *Holy Place.* After that he took a censer with hot coals on it into the Holy of Holies. There he threw incense on the coals that the smoke of it might cover the mercy seat (vv. 12-13). This suggests prayer as he approached the mercy seat, "that he die not" (v. 13) in approaching so holy a place. Taking the blood of the bullock he again entered the Holy of Holies where he sprinkled blood on the mercy seat, and then seven times before it (v. 14). The two goats were up to this time kept outside the tabernacle (v. 7). One was to be a sin offering to Jehovah; the other to be the scapegoat or *Azazel.* So now he took the one to be sacrificed to Jehovah for the sins of the people (v. 15). Killing it, he carried its blood into the Holy of Holies and sprinkled it as he had done with the bullock's blood. Also he made a similar atonement for the Holy Place (vv. 16-19). Then symbolically he placed the sins of the people on the head of the scapegoat which was led away into the wilderness, thus bearing away the people's sins (vv. 20-22).

The high priest then entered the Holy Place where he discarded the linen garments, leaving them there, washed himself, and put on his regular garments. With this done he offered the ram as a burnt offering for himself and the people. The fat of the ram also was burned on the altar (vv. 24-25).

The one leading the scapegoat away was required to wash his clothes and body before returning to the camp (v. 26). The skins, flesh, and dung of the bullock and goat were burned outside the camp. The one doing this was also required to wash his clothes and body before returning to the camp (vv. 27-28).

Franz Delitzsch has called the Day of Atonement "the Good Friday of the Old Testament," which relates it to its fulfilment in Christ. The Old Testament Day of Atonement was "the figures [copy] of the true" (Heb. 9:24).

The author of Hebrews shows how the repeated observance of this day under the old covenant was fulfilled in the once-for-all sacrifice of Christ (Heb. 9:1-10). He is both the high priest and the sacrifice. Sinless, he needed no atonement for himself before coming into God's presence. "But Christ being come an high priest of good things to come, by a greater and more perfect tabernacle, not made with hands, that is to say, not of this building; neither by the blood of goats and calves, but by his own blood he entered in once into the holy place, having obtained eternal [not annual] redemption for us" (Heb. 9:11-12).

Thus he is "the mediator of the new testament" or covenant. (Heb. 9:15). For a testament or will to be effective, the testator must die (v. 16). The old covenant under Moses was sealed with animals' blood—unwilling and unknowing sacrifices. But Christ gave himself knowingly and willingly as an atonement for our sins.

"For Christ is not entered into the holy places [note the plural, Holy Place and Holy of Holies] made with hands, which are the figures [types] of the true: but into heaven itself, now to appear in the presence of God for [as our substitute, on our behalf, see Isa. 53:4-7] us: not that he should offer himself often, as the high priest entereth into the holy place every year with blood of others . . . but now once in the end of the world hath he appeared to put away sin by the sacrifice of himself" (Heb. 9:24-26). Thus he is "the Lamb of God, which taketh away the sin of the world" (John 1:29)!

Augustus. Augustus was the first Roman emperor (27 B.C. to A.D. 14). His original name was Caius Octavius Caepias. Born in 63 B.C., he was the grand-nephew of Julius Caesar. Out of the turmoil following the murder of Julius Caesar (44 B.C.), he finally emerged without a rival following his victory at Actium in 31 B.C. He declined to be called *rex* or *dictator*. But in 27 B.C. the Roman Senate called him Augustus. This name implied respect and veneration beyond that given to mere men (see *Emperor Worship*).

Augustus figures in the New Testament record as the ruling emperor when Jesus was born (Luke 2:1). Luke follows the practice of dating events by the reign of people at the time. Augustus in 8 B.C. inaugurated a system of enrolment for taxation every fourteen years. With a few gaps records of these periodic enrolments have been found extending into the latter half of the third century. It was the first of these enrolments, probably delayed by Herod the Great to placate the Jews, which furnished the occasion for

Joseph and Mary to be in Bethlehem at the time of Jesus' birth in 6 or 5 B.C. Unknowingly this pagan emperor was used of God in fulfilment of prophecy as to the place of Christ's birth (Mic. 5:2).

Babbler. In Acts 17:18 "babbler" translates a Greek word which was used of a bird which picked up seeds. It was used by the Epicurean and Stoic philosophers to refer to Paul. Apparently he had been going from place to place in the Athenian marketplace talking about Jesus and the resurrection to any who would listen. So in a sense the philosophers in contempt called him a "seed-picker."

The word was also used of one who made his living by picking up odds and ends from merchants and selling them. Thus a parasite. In the literary sense it denoted a plagiarist who used other people's ideas without the capacity to use them correctly (Sir William Ramsey, *St. Paul the Traveller and Roman Citizen,* pp. 141ff.). Thus the philosophers accused Paul of plagiarism, using other people's ideas but with no system of thought of his own. They really described themselves. On Mar's Hill they learned differently about Paul.

Babylon. This city was the capital of the Babylonian empire which destroyed Jerusalem in 587 B.C. and took many citizens of Judah into the seventy-year captivity. "Babylon" in the book of Revelation (17:5; 18:2) is probably used as a symbol of Rome.

Balaam. He is mentioned in Numbers 22:2 to 24:5 as one who sought to place a curse on Israel for personal gain, but was prevented by God from doing so. Second Peter 2:15 uses him as an example of evil teachers. Revelation 2:14 mentions those holding "the doctrine of Balaam." These were probably those who taught Christians to live according to the flesh, to compromise with the world, probably to escape Roman persecution.

Baptism. The English word "baptize" is a transliteration of the Greek verb *baptizō.* In all Greek lexicons it is defined to mean to dip, plunge, submerge, or immerse. The Greek language has words for "sprinkle" and "pour." But they are never used in the New Testament in the sense of *baptism.*

In Jewish ritualism "baptize" was used for the ceremonial bath designed to cleanse one from pollution (see Lev. 15:16). It was also used for ceremonial dipping of eating utensils (Mark 7:4b). However, this has no direct relationship with Christian baptism. This verb was also used as a metaphor in the sense of being overwhelmed in trouble (Mark 10:38-39). It is used to express the work of the Holy Spirit in creating the fellowship of believers as in the body of Christ (1 Cor. 12:13).

The baptism of John the Baptist was symbolic of repentance from sin and willingness to participate in the kingdom of God (Matt. 3:2,6,11a). Since Jesus had no sin of which to repent, his baptism (Matt. 3:13-17) is usually understood to mean severally: his authentification of John's message; his identity with other men; the inauguration of his ministry; symbolic prophecy of his redemptive work through his death, burial, and resurrection. That Christian baptism has a different significance from John's baptism is seen in Acts 19:1-5.

Christian baptism is the immersion of a believer in Christ in water and his emergence from water. It is not a sacrament but a symbol. It symbolizes what Christ did for one's salvation: his death, burial, and resurrection; what he does in the believer: death of the old life, its burial, and his resurrection to a new life in Christ; and the believer's faith in the resurrection of the body at the Lord's return (Rom. 6:3-5). Thus, assuming a believer, New Testament baptism involves a proper meaning and a proper mode to express that meaning. If either the meaning or mode be altered, baptism loses its significance. Thus even immersion as a means to salvation does not correspond to the New Testament *meaning* (see *Baptismal Regeneration*). Pouring or sprinkling for baptism and infant baptism grew out of a later belief that baptism was necessary for salvation. It was a gradual development in the West, culminating in the Council of Trent (Roman Catholic) which decreed that sprinkling constituted baptism. The Eastern or Greek Orthodox Church, following its knowledge of the Greek language, continues to use immersion as its form of baptism.

The noun forms rendered "baptism" are *baptismos* and *baptisma*. The former is never used in the New Testament to refer to Christian baptism. It refers to Jewish ceremonial cleansings (Mark 7:4b; Heb. 6:2; 9:10). The latter word refers to the meaning in the act of baptism (see *Baptismal Regeneration*). It is the term translated "baptism" in all but the above references. This word does not appear in any Greek writings except the New Testament and subsequent ecclesiastical writings which borrowed from the New Testament usage. Evidently this word was coined to express the meaning in Christian baptism. For a full discussion of various views on "Baptism" see *The International Standard Bible Encyclopaedia* (Grand Rapids: Eerdmans, 1949, edited by James Orr, Volume I), pages 385-401.

Baptismal Regeneration. This view holds that baptism is a sacrament, not simply a symbol, or is necessary for salvation. In the early Christian centuries it gave rise to clinical baptism or baptism of the sick, and infant baptism. Gradually these practices led to pouring and sprinkling as modes of *baptism.*

This doctrinal position is based upon certain passages which are interpreted thus. Space does not permit an exhaustive treatment of all these. However, the preponderance of passages concerning salvation which make no mention of baptism suggests caution at this point. Jesus did all that is necessary for man's salvation, yet he himself baptized no one (John 4:2). Paul insisted that in Corinth he baptized only a small number of people (1 Cor. 1:14-17a). Four verses are worthy of examination.

(1) Mark 16:16. New Testament scholarship agrees that the oldest and best manuscripts of Mark end with 16:8. Various later manuscripts have different endings. It is concluded that Mark 16:9-20 is not genuine Scripture. Within itself verse 16b makes no mention of baptism, which makes this verse suspect.

(2) John 3:5. The mention of being "born of water" does not necessarily imply baptism. It may refer to spiritual cleansing. Or it may refer to the natural birth which is accompanied by water. The sense of verses 3-7 seems to be Jesus' effort to contrast the natural with the spiritual birth.

(3) Acts 2:38. The meaning here hinges on "for." Does it mean result or cause? The Greek preposition may mean for, into, unto, because of, on the basis of, with respect to, or as a result of. In

Matthew 12:41; Luke 11:32 it is rendered "at." The Ninevites did not repent in order that Jonah might preach but as the result of his preaching. In English "for" is used in the same sense. "He was executed for murder." Not that he might murder but that he had already murdered. Baptism is not in order that one's sins may be remitted but because they have already been remitted. This same preposition is rendered "into" in Romans 6:3-4. Perhaps a better reading here would be "with respect to."

(4) 1 Peter 3:20-21. The word rendered "baptism" in verse 21 is *baptisma,* the meaning in the act of baptism, not the act itself (see *Baptism*). The eight souls were saved not "by" but "through" *(dia)* water. They were saved not by being *in* the water but *through* the flood by being in the ark, corresponding to Christ. This figure and its meaning are symbolized by *baptisma* or baptism.

James Orr (ISBE, Vol. 1, p. 397) says of baptism, "It is the symbol of a cleansing from sin and renewal by God's Spirit, but not the agency effecting that renewal, even instrumentally . . . In Scripture the agency with which regeneration is specially connected is the Divine 'Word' (cf. 1 Pet. 1:23)." Thus baptism does not contribute toward one entering the kingdom of God. It is an act of obedience which admits the believer into the fellowship of the local church with its rights, privileges, and responsibilities. It is the former of two church ordinances (see *Lord's Supper*).

Baptism for the Dead. This belief is based upon one verse of Scripture (1 Cor. 15:29) where Paul is discussing the bodily resurrection. It is of uncertain meaning as seen in over fifty efforts to interpret it. The first mention of being "baptized for the dead" is found in the writings of Tertullian, who understood Paul to refer to a practice of vicarious baptism or living Christians being baptized on behalf of dead people who had not been baptized. This reflects the belief that baptism is essential for salvation. Later Epiphanius and Chrysostom mention such a custom among the Epicureans and Marcionites respectively. This reflects the belief of Tertullian.

"The dead" is ambiguous. It could refer to dead people or to those dead to sin who in baptism symbolize their spiritual experience. Since no other New Testament passage mentions such a practice on behalf of dead people, the writer is inclined to regard "the dead" as referring to the Christians who died to sin, were buried, and raised to a new life in Christ.

Therefore, the meaning could be that if there be no resurrection, why should the believer submit to baptism as a symbol of his salvation experience and faith in the bodily resurrection? Thus Paul argues that even Christian baptism reflects one's belief in his future bodily resurrection.

Baptism of the Holy Spirit. In Matthew 3:11 John the Baptist said that Jesus would baptize in the Holy Spirit and in fire. Most likely this refers to his cleansing from sin and consuming the dross of such; to light the flame of divine love and enthusiasm; to illuminate Christians with divine understanding of the Scriptures. It involves the action of the Spirit upon, and his entering into, the lives of those who believe in Jesus. In John 14:17 Jesus said to his disciples that the Holy Spirit indwells believers (cf. 1 Cor. 6:19; 2 Cor. 1:22; Eph. 1:13-14).

The Holy Spirit indwells the human spirit. As the human spirit indwells the body it is thus that he indwells the believer. As he indwells those who compose the church fellowship, he also indwells the church (1 Cor. 3:16). Paul calls both the Christian's body and the church fellowship the "temple" or Holy of Holies of the Holy Spirit.

At Pentecost the Holy Spirit came upon the church in Jerusalem in power (Acts 2:1-4). Elsewhere in Acts where the Spirit comes upon individuals it is always in connection with their regeneration experience (8:15-17; 10:44; 19:6). This is not an evidence of *sanctification* as interpreted by those who hold to the "second blessing," but of regeneration. Paul says, "Now if any man have not the Spirit of Christ, he is none of his" (Rom. 8:9). So the Holy Spirit in the Christian's life is not an *extra* blessing but a necessity. His presence is not for a spiritually elite group but for all believers (1 Cor. 12:13).

Thus it appears that the "second blessing" is not supported by the New Testament. What some see as such is perhaps some signal religious experience in which the individual yields himself afresh to the power of the Spirit who already indwells him. Thus one may in the course of his Christian life have not simply the first and second blessings, but perhaps a thousand blessings. The old adage is true. The Christian possesses all of the Holy Spirit. The question is as to how much of him the Holy Spirit possesses.

Barbarian; Barbarous (Greek, *barbaros*). These terms were used by the Greeks to refer to all other people who did not follow Greek culture and speak the Greek language. Any other language to them sounded like *bar bar,* so *barbaros.* Thus in Romans 1:14 "Greeks . . . Barbarians" refers to the entire human race. In 1 Corinthians 14:11 "barbarian" means a person speaking any language other than Greek. In Colossians 3:11 Paul uses it in connection with "Scythian." In this usage "barbarian" carries its usual meaning. "Scythian" is climactic referring to the lowest kind of "barbarians." Paul's point is that in Christ all human distinctions disappear (cf. Gal. 3:28).

In Acts 28:2,4 the terms "barbarous" and "barbarian" appear. Both translate the plural form of *barbaros (barbaroi).* With the definite article they mean "the barbarians." Thus "barbarous" does not mean *cruel* as the context plainly shows. Luke used these terms to refer to them as non-Greeks.

Bar-Jonah. Since the word "Bar" is used often in the New Testament in combination with proper names, a brief word about it is helpful. It is the Aramaic (language spoken by Jesus in Palestine in the first century) for "son," the equivalent of the Hebrew *bēn.* Note Barnabas (son of consolation, Acts 4:36), Barabbas (son of father, John 18:14), and Bartholomew (son of Tolmai, Matt. 10:3).

Its most notable use is in connection with Simon Peter. John 1:42 reads "Simon, the son [Greek, *huios*] of John." John used this word rather than the Aramaic *Bar* in favor of his Greek readers. Three times in John 21:15-17 the best Greek texts read simply "Simon of John." But in Matthew 16:17 the reading is "Simon Bar-jona." Either Simon's father had two names—John and Jonah—or else "Jonah" *(Iōnas)* may be a contraction of "John" *(Iōanēs),* probably the latter. In modern parlance he would be called "Simon Johnson."

Beam. In the New Testament this word appears only in the Sermon on the Mount (Matt. 7:3-5; Luke 6:41-42). The Greek word so translated means a large piece of wood such as a pole or rafter. It is contrasted with a "mote," something very small like a speck of dirt or dust. The figure is that of a "hypocrite" (Matt. 7:5; Luke 6:42) or censorious person who picks at the little faults of others while ignoring his greater sins. One sees here an element of Jesus' humor as he pictures one with a large beam sticking out of his own eye as he tries to pick a small speck out of another's eye.

Beast. This word is of interest in Christian doctrine because of two Greek words used to denote such in Revelation. For instance, one word rendered "beast" is found referring to "four beasts" before God's throne in heaven (Rev. 4:6-7; 5:8,11,14; cf. also 6:1-8). This probably symbolizes a redeemed natural order, as the twenty-four elders connote a redeemed spiritual order (Rev. 4:4,10-11; 5:8,11,14).

The other word for "beast" means a wild, ferocious beast (cf. Rev. 11:7; 13:1-2,11; 15:2; 16:13; 17:8,11; 19:19; 20:10). This beast is used to refer to the Roman empire or to the Roman emperor Domitian. This beast receives its power from the dragon Satan (Rev. 13:2). See *Beast, The Mark of the.*

Beast, The Mark of the. This mark or "number" is found in Revelation 13:18. The number of the beast is the number of a man: 666. The beast is described in Revelation 13:1-8; cf. vv. 11-17. Interpreters differ as to the identity of the beast. One group sees it as the Antichrist. The writer belongs to the school of thought which identifies the "beast . . . out of the sea" (v. 1) as imperial Rome personified in the emperor Domitian. This power crossed the sea and invaded Asia or Asia Minor (the Roman province of Asia). The "beast . . . out of the earth" (v. 11) is the Roman Concilia, a local body charged with enforcing emperor-worship. But since the beast in verse 18 is identified with a man, it must refer to Domitian.

Revelation is an apocalypse or unveiling. This type of writing in symbols was used by Jews in time of trouble. Knowing the symbolism, they could communicate with each other but conceal the message from their enemies. Numerology played a great part in this type of writing (see *Numbers*). In primitive languages letters were used as numerals; cf. Roman V = 5. So using various languages

(Hebrew, Greek, Latin) 666 has been identified as Nero Caesar, Roman Catholic Church, or the pope. Such results show how futile these efforts are.

It seems, therefore, that the significance lies in the number itself. Numbers also had a meaning. For instance, *one* symbolized unity, *two* strength or courage; *three* was the number of deity, a perfect number. *Seven* suggested completeness or perfection. Since *six* fell short of *seven,* it meant incompleteness or imperfection. So *6* would symbolize imperfect or evil. Three *sixes* (666) would be a perfect number of imperfections or complete evil. John's use symbolizes everything brutal, evil, and terrible. Domitian who then was persecuting the Christians typified complete evil. Had John used his name, it would have been disaster for him and many other Christians. But by using this number he got his message across to his readers.

Another possibility is in order: *6* is evil. Here it is raised to the number *3*, the number of deity. So the idea could be that an evil man as a tool of Satan (v. 4) sought to raise himself to the level of a god.

John could have said no more terrible thing about Domitian than to give him the number "666." Literally, "Here is wisdom. The one having intelligence in oriental numerology let him count the number of the beast; for it is the number of a man" (v. 18).

Beatitudes. The word "beatitude" does not appear in the English versions of the Bible. It comes from the Latin *beatitudo* which is used in the Vulgate version of Romans 4:6. Since the time of Ambrose the name Beatitudes has referred to Jesus' words in Matthew 5:3-12 and Luke 6:20-26 which begin their versions of the Sermon on the Mount. However, a comparison between them shows certain differences. For instance, Matthew has eight and Luke four followed by four "woes." Matthew's are spiritual in nature; Luke's are more material. The former are longer and smoother than the latter.

Some scholars explain these differences by placing them on different occasions. But the context of each seems to rule otherwise. Others see them as derived from different sources, with Luke's shorter and rougher form being the manner in which they were spoken by Jesus. Generally in literary criticism this would be the favored position.

However, this writer suggests another view, with Matthew's being the older and truer form. Luke says that he derived his material from other sources both oral and written (Luke 1:1-4). He recorded them as they were given to him. Matthew was present when Jesus spoke them. As a former tax collector he was accustomed to keeping records. He could have been adept at shorthand which was available then. In any case he preserved the beatitudes, perhaps verbatim or in practically the form Jesus gave them. This could account for the smooth diction even throughout the Sermon. At any rate, the substance of both accounts is the same.

Since "Beatitudes" is usually associated in popular thought with Matthew's account, an analysis of it proves helpful. Jesus is setting forth the qualities of citizens of the kingdom of God. The writer sees them as a progressive experience in the individual believer's life.

Verse 3 describes the "poor in spirit," or one who is spiritually poverty stricken. Nothing in him is worthy of kingdom citizenship. Hence, *conviction* of sin. Such is ready to enter the kingdom by God's grace.

Verse 4 speaks of those who "mourn" as for the dead. Hence, *repentance*.

Verse 5 describes the "meek" or teachable one who enrols as Jesus' disciple. Thus, *faith*.

Verse 6 describes one who hungers and thirsts for righteousness. As God's child he has these deepest of longings for a greater experience with God. So, *sanctification*.

Verse 7 refers to the "merciful." As God has forgiven him so he forgives others. Hence, *Christian love*.

Verse 8 describes the "peacemakers." At peace with God, he seeks to lead others to the same condition. Thus, the *missionary motive*.

Verses 10-11 show that such will be persecuted and reviled by the world—for Jesus' name's sake. But they are to rejoice in that they are in good company—the prophets. Thus, *victorious living for Christ*.

William Barclay makes an interesting suggestion. The feminine form of the word rendered "blessed" was used to describe Cyprus as "the happy isle." It was said to be so rich in natural resources that one could be born, live, and die on it—never leaving it—and yet live a rich, full life. In Jesus Christ the Christian finds all he needs for the abundant life (John 10:10).

Bethany. Bethany, meaning "house of figs," figures prominently in the Judean ministry of Jesus. It has been called his *home* in Judea (Matt. 21:17; Mark 11:11). While Luke 10:38 does not name the village, it is evident that Jesus' visit to the home of Martha took place in Bethany (John 11:1). This seems to have been his favorite lodging place while in the area of Jerusalem (John 11:3). The village was located just over the crest of the Mount of Olives eastward from Jerusalem, a little less than two miles from the city.

It was the scene of Jesus' greatest miracle, the raising of Lazarus from the dead (John 11:1-45). Here also Jesus was the dinner guest in the home of Simon the leper (Matt. 26:6-13; Mark 14:3-9; John 12:1-8). It was at this dinner that Mary of Bethany anointed Jesus beforehand for his burial (John 12:3-7), an act which is a perpetual memorial to her love for him (Matt. 26:13; Mark 14:8-9). Also it was here that Judas finally resolved to betray Jesus (Matt. 26:14-16; Mark 14:10-11). It was from near Bethany that Jesus ascended into heaven (Luke 24:50-51).

Bethany today is called *el'Azarēyeh,* the place of Lazarus. It is a poor village facing east on the southeastern slope of the Mount of Olives. Whether authentic or not, tourists still are shown the home of Martha, Mary, and Lazarus and the traditional tomb of Lazarus.

Bethesda, Pool of. The best Greek texts read *Bethzatha.* The exact location of the pool of Bethesda (house of mercy) has long been in question. It has been identified at several locations, but mainly as the Virgin's Fountain which even today has intermittent troubling of the water. However, this does not fit the description of John 5:2. John locates it at the place of the sheep. Nehemiah 3:1,32; 12:39 mentions such a place. Late in the nineteenth century the ruins of two Christian churches were discovered near this place. These had been built over a twin pool, suggesting that it was regarded as a sacred site. From the fourth century A.D. probably until the time of the Crusades this had been pointed out as the place of the pool of Bethesda. But for some reason it was not excavated. It is located near the Church of St. Anne, just north and slightly west of the Temple area.

However, in recent years this site has been partially excavated. It shows two parallel pools with a stone separation between them. This could explain the "five porches" mentioned by John: one on each side of the pools with a fifth resting on the area which separates them. The location is exactly where John places it, and most likely is the pool of Bethesda. Incidently, this argues for the author of the Fourth Gospel being a native of Palestine and one familiar with Jerusalem prior to its destruction by the Romans in A.D. 70. It argues for John the Apostle as the author.

It was here that Jesus healed the man who had been lame for thirty-eight years (John 5:5-9). Of interest is the fact that verse 4 is not in the oldest and best manuscripts of John. It was added by a later hand, probably reflecting an old Jewish superstition.

Betray. See *Judas Iscariot.*

Bible, The. The word "Bible" comes from the Greek *biblia* meaning "books." The Bible is composed of the Old Testament (39 books) and the New Testament (27 books). The New Testament references to the Scriptures refer to the Old Testament, sometimes called, the "scriptures," "the law and the prophets" or "the law, the prophets, and the writings." The last word includes Psalms, Wisdom Literature (Job, Proverbs, Ecclesiastes, Song of Solomon), and certain of the historical books. The books of the New Testament were gradually included in the Canon of Scripture, the process culminating in the fourth century A.D. in the councils of Laodicea (about A.D. 363) and Carthage (A.D. 397).

The Old Testament was written largely in Hebrew, with certain additions of Aramaic and brief evidences of other languages. The New Testament was written entirely in Greek, with an occasional word of Aramaic or Latin origin. Aramaic was the language spoken by the Palestinian Jews of the first century. The Greek of the New Testament differs from classical Greek. At one time it was thought to be a special language given of God to use in writing the New

Testament. One scholar even called it "the language of the Holy Ghost." It is now known to be the language found in the papyri (writings of the ordinary concourse of life: for instance: deeds, contracts, letters, commercial papers). Thus it is now called the *Koine* or common Greek. Uses in the papyri throw great light on the New Testament usage. All but about fifty words in the New Testament have been found in the papyri.

The Bible was written over a period of about fifteen hundred years, places of writing ranging all the way from Babylon to Rome. Its writers included, among others, kings, peasants, shepherds, farmers, poets, prophets, fishermen, a former tax collector, a physician, and apostles. No one knew he was writing a part of the *Bible*. Yet when the books were gathered together they comprise a whole. If one read the Old Testament, having no knowledge of the New, he would ask as to the rest of it. Conversely, if one read the New Testament, with no knowledge of the Old, he would ask as to that which preceded it. The New Testament is the flower of the Old Testament. The Old Testament should be interpreted in the light of the New. The criterion for interpreting the Bible is God's full revelation in Jesus Christ.

This unity of the Bible can be explained only by seeing one Author for the whole. And this Author is God through his Holy Spirit (2 Tim. 3:16-17; 2 Pet. 1:21, see *Revelation, Inspiration, and Illumination*). It is the written Word of God about his living Word, without any mixture of error for its matter.

The Bible is not primarily a book of history, philosophy, or science. Yet it contains history found nowhere else. It is history within history or holy history. It is the history of God's redeeming purpose for man and the universe. No historical error has ever been proved against it. When archaeology has spoken on questioned passages, it has supported the Bible. It teaches a divine philosophy of history, man, nature, and the universe. Although written in the popular language of people and of its time, no scientific error has been proved against it. Interpreters of the Bible and scientific *theories* may differ. But when both the Bible and science are fully understood, they agree. All *truth* is of God—whether it be found in the Bible or in natural phenomena. And God does not contradict himself.

Primarily the Bible is a book of religion. It reveals God and his will to man. It presents man in his true nature as one created in God's image: his original innocence, sin and fall, and God's purpose and provision to redeem him from sin and restore him to divine fellowship.

No other book has been subjected to critical scrutiny as has the Bible. Yet it has won the battle. The more man learns about the Bible the stronger its position becomes. No one needs to discard his intellect when he avows his faith in the Bible. It does not ask to be defended but read, used, and proclaimed. As one has said, "I know the Bible is God's inspired Word because it finds me at a deeper level than any other book."

Bishop. See *Elder*.

Blood. Blood is important in the Bible. Old Testament law made no provision for forgiveness "without the shedding of blood" (Heb. 9:22).

The first mention of blood in the Bible is found in Genesis 4:9. But the shedding of blood is implied in God's providing "coats of skin" to cover the nakedness of Adam and Eve (Gen. 3:21), and may be involved in the difference between the offerings of Abel and Cain. It is a foregleam of the truth that man's sin is covered by the shedding of blood.

Primitive man learned from what he saw. He noted that when blood flowed from the body of animal or man the result was death. So he reasoned that somehow life was in the blood. This is echoed in Leviticus 17:14. Because life is in the blood it is forbidden that man should eat blood (cf. Gen. 9:4). This reflects the pagan custom of drinking the blood of sacrificial victims, thinking thereby to receive the life which flowed from the animal. So ages before William Harvey in 1615 discovered the circulation of blood, its life-giving properties were known to the ancients.

In the Hebrew sacrificial system animal blood foretold the cleansing power from sin. Doctor Jack Hough, noted physician of Oklahoma City, Oklahoma, said in the presence of the writer that blood is the most effective cleansing agent known to medical science. This but reflects the spiritual efficacy of blood to cleanse from sin. Serum made from the blood of those who have been cured of certain diseases is effective in treating others having the same diseases. The practice of blood transfusion, especially the use of blood plasma, speaks to the life-giving qualities of blood. One physician noted that if blood is prescribed there can be no substitute for it.

These facts, plus the system of animal sacrifice in the Old Testament, but enhance the place of Christ's blood in God's redemptive purpose. (See *Atonement* and *Atonement, Day of.*) When Christ gave his blood he gave his life (John 10:11). And because he lives, those who believe in him shall live also (John 14:19). For "the blood of Jesus Christ his Son cleanseth us from all sin" (1 John 1:7; cf. 1 Pet. 1:18-19).

Book of Life. This phrase is based upon the ancient custom of keeping genealogical records (Neh. 7:5, 64) and of enroling citizens for various reasons (Ezek. 13:9). Thus God is seen as having a record of his own people who are under his care. To be blotted out of the Book of Life is to be removed from God's favor and protection, to die an untimely death, as in the case of Moses who prayed to be blotted out of God's book or that he might die in order to save Israel from punishment (Exod. 32:32; Psalm 69:28).

In the New Testament this Book refers to those who through faith in Jesus Christ are to inherit eternal life (Phil. 4:3; Rev. 3:5; 13:8; 17:8; 20:12,15; 21:27). Of course, one should not see a literal book. The Holy Spirit uses human custom to express the truth that the Lord's people are known to him. If men can store up data in a computer, who can deny the infinite knowledge of God in which his own are known to him? See *Judgment, Last.*

Born Again. See *Salvation.*

Brethren of Jesus. The Greek word rendered "brother" comes from another meaning "out of the same womb." The feminine form is translated "sister" (Mark 6:3). While teaching in Nazareth the hometown folks were astonished that one from there could possess such knowledge. They asked, "Is not this the carpenter, the son of Mary, the brother of James, and Joses [Joseph], and of Juda [Jude], and Simon? and are not his sisters here with us?" (Mark 6:3; see Matt. 13:55-56). John 2:12 mentions Jesus' brothers as traveling with him from Cana (or Nazareth) to Capernaum. On one occasion during his Galilean ministry his mother and brothers came to see him (Matt. 12:46-47; see also Mark 3:31-32; Luke 8:19-20). John 7:5 says that his brothers did not believe in him as the Christ. They did not believe in him until after the resurrection and his appearance to James (1 Cor. 15:7). Along with Mary, Jesus' brothers were in the group which awaited the coming of the Holy Spirit at Pentecost (Acts 1:14).

Later James became the leader or pastor of the church in Jerusalem (Acts 15). In Galatians 1:19 Paul calls him "the Lord's brother." He was the author of the book of James, as Jude was of the one called by his name. Of interest is the fact that neither presumes upon this family relationship. Each calls himself a "servant" or slave of Jesus Christ (James 1:1; Jude 1). But Jude does call himself "brother of James" (Jude 1). Apparently they responded to Jesus' earlier words that one's relationship to him was not genetical but spiritual. "Who is my mother? and who are my brethren? And he stretched forth his hand toward his disciples, and said, Behold my mother and my brethren! For whosoever shall do the will of my Father which is in heaven, the same is my brother, and sister, and mother" (Matt. 12:48-50).

Through the years those holding to the perpetual virginity of Mary have sought to explain the "brethren" of Jesus in two ways: that they are children of Joseph by a former marriage; or Jesus' stepbrothers or that the word "brethren" may be understood as "kinsmen" or "cousins." However, the arguments for these positions, though ancient, are inconclusive. The statement in Matthew 1:25 clearly implies that after Jesus' birth Joseph and Mary lived in normal marital relations. Furthermore, "firstborn son" in Luke 2:7 (not genuine in Matt. 1:25) clearly means that there were other children born to the union of Joseph and Mary.

Since the Gospels of Matthew and Luke clearly teach the virgin birth of Jesus (see *Virgin Birth*), those mentioned as Jesus' brothers and sisters were his half-brothers and half-sisters. This idea is true to the overall teaching of the Scriptures.

Bridegroom. See *Marriage.*

Burden. This English word is of interest because it appears twice in Galatians 6:2,5 in a seeming contradiction. However, the harmony between the two is clear in the Greek text.

"Bear ye one another's burdens, and so fulfil the law of Christ" (v. 2). The reference here and in verse 5 is to moral weaknesses, but the lesson may be extended to other phases of life. The word rendered "burdens" *(baros)* means something heavy, the burden of the day (Matt. 20:12), or the burden of duty or a difficult requirement to be borne (Acts 15:28; Rev. 2:24).

"For every man shall bear his own burden" (v. 5). Here the "burden" *(phortion)* is a burden to be borne (Matt. 11:30; Luke 11:46). It speaks of one's individual responsibility. One likens it to a soldier's pack which he alone should bear regardless of its weight.

Perhaps the difference between these burdens is one of degree. The one in verse 2 is a load so heavy that without help it will crush the bearer. In such case Christians should help one another, thus fulfilling the law of Christ and Christian care and love. But the burden in verse 5 is one, however heavy, which a person alone can bear. So in this case the Christian should bear his own burden and not sponge on others.

If the burden be a moral problem, then one must play the man in shouldering his own responsibility. It is only then that others can lend a hand if it proves to be a burden such as seen in verse 2. If it be, for instance, a burden of sorrow, there is a limit to which others can go in helping such. The same is true in poverty. Until one is willing to do his best, the help of others will avail little. But when one has reached the limit of his own power, then others should step in to lend a hand.

Caesarea; Caesarea Philippi. In Jesus' time there were two cities in Palestine which bore the name Caesarea. The Greek word means "of Caesar" or "Caesar's town" or city.

(1) The original Caesarea was located on the Mediterranean coast some thirty miles north of Joppa. Present-day excavation of the site reveals remarkable Roman ruins. This city was built by Herod the Great on the site of Strato's Tower. He named it Caesarea and its port Sebastos in honor of Caesar Augustus. Included among

its spacious buildings (palaces, public buildings, and a theater) was a temple to Augustus. Its large amphitheater (seating 20,000) facing the sea has been restored. It was in this amphitheater that Agrippa I was stricken and later died (Acts 12:19-23). The city even had an underground sewerage system.

One of the greatest features of the city was its excellent harbor made by sinking stones 50x18x9 into water twenty fathoms deep. It required twelve years to build the city which was finished in 10-9 B.C.

In Jesus' time it was the residence of the Roman procurator. For a brief time it was held by Agrippa I. But after his death the procurators resumed residence there.

Caesarea figures in the Christian story as seen in Acts. It was the home of Philip the evangelist (8:40; 21:8). Here Peter preached the gospel for the first time to non-Jews (Acts 10). (Cornelius was a "God-fearer," a Gentile studying Judaism but had not become a Jew in religion, 10:2; see *Proselyte*). Paul sailed either out or into Palestine here four times (9:30; 18:22; 21:8; 27:2). He spent two years in prison there (23:23 to 26:32). While there he appeared before Felix, Festus, Herod Agrippa II, and his sister-wife Bernice. It was in Caesarea that Paul made his appeal to appear before Caesar (Acts 25:11-12,25). This resulted in his two years' imprisonment in his own hired house in Rome (Acts 28:30).

(2) Caesarea Philippi. This city was so called to distinguish it from Caesarea by the sea. It means Caesarea of Philip, a son of Herod the Great. This city was located at the base of Mount Hermon. One may still see there a cave in which pagans said the Greek god Pan was born. Thus it was a center of this god's worship. Hence it was at one time called Paneas, a name which survives in the present name Banias for a small village located there. It may have been the ancient site of Dan, a center of Israelite worship.

The area was given by Augustus to Herod the Great in 20 B.C. He built there a temple to the emperor. Herod Philip rebuilt and beautified it, naming it Caesarea in honor of Augustus. Later Agrippa II named it Neronias in honor of Nero.

It was in this area that Peter made his confession of Jesus as "the Christ, the Son of the living God" (Matt. 16:16). Since this area was historically related to Jewish and pagan worship, including emperor worship, it was a fitting place for Jesus to test his disciples as to their concept of him. Near here may be seen today the carvings of ancient rulers, the identity of some being obscure even then. One can almost see the disciples guessing as to their identity when Jesus asked, "Whom say ye that I am?" (Matt. 16:15). Probably near here also Jesus was transfigured (Matt. 17:1-9). See *Church* and *Transfiguration.*

Calvary. See *Golgotha.*

Christ. See *Jesus Christ.*

Christ, Anti; Antichrist. "Antichrist" should not be confused with the false Christs *(pseudochristoi)* mentioned by Jesus in Matthew 24:5, 24. These are false teachers or leaders who claim to be Christ. "Antichrist" is just what it says. It is *anti Christ (antichristos).*

The word "antichrist" appears in the New Testament only in 1 John 2:18,22; 4:3; 2 John 7. In 1 John 2:18 it appears twice without the definite article, so simply "antichrist" or "an antichrist." All other references have the definite article, so "the antichrist." However, John does not seem to point to any one particular person. His reference is to one or more who deny that Jesus Christ has come in the flesh. Evidently he is talking about Gnostic philosophers. One group, the Docetic Gnostics, held that Christ did not have a real flesh-and-blood body, but only *seemed* to have. "Docetic" comes from the Greek *dokeō,* I seem. They denied the humanity of Christ. The other group, the Cerinthians, from the name of their leader Cerinthus, said that Christ was neither born nor did he die. He came upon Jesus at his baptism (Matt. 3:16) and left him on the cross (Matt. 27:46 where they rendered "God" as "Power"). Thus they denied the deity of Jesus. Both, says John, were anti-Christ. In this sense anyone who denies the deity/humanity of Jesus Christ is an antichrist or the antichrist. Thus anyone who opposes Christ is *antichrist.*

However, "the Antichrist" is by many applied to "the man of sin" or "lawlessness" (best texts) mentioned by Paul in 2 Thessalonians 2:3-10. He says that Christ will not return until after this "man of lawlessness" is revealed. This one works by the power of Satan (v. 9). Some relate this person to Daniel 7:7-8 who will be destroyed by Christ (7:13-14). Others equate this with Antiochus Epiphanes who ruled over the Seleucid kingdom 175-164 B.C. (Dan. 8:9-12,23-25). But this does not seem to fit the idea of Antichrist.

Paul's "man of lawlessness" is described as one who opposes God and exalts himself above all that is called God, is worshiped, calls himself God, and sits in the temple of God (2 Thess. 2:4). Some associate this with the Roman emperor Caligula who claimed to be God and ordered that his image be placed in the temple in Jerusalem. But he reigned A.D. 37-41, before Paul wrote 2 Thessalonians. The "man of lawlessness" is in the future from the time of Paul's writing. Some relate this figure to Nero, Domitian, or other Roman emperors who demanded that they be worshiped as gods. The Roman Catholic papacy is seen by some to fulfil this prophecy. Other figures at different times in history have been equated with this person. For example, Hitler. Which shows the difficulty of identifying him at any given period in history.

The apostle further states that "the man of lawlessness" is being prevented from appearing until "his time" (2 Thess. 2:6). He is already at work, but is being restrained by another power about which Paul's readers know (2 Thess. 5,7). Some see "he who now letteth" or holds down as the emperor Claudius (A.D. 41-54). However, it seems more likely that this refers to the system of orderly government which restrains an absolutely lawless one.

In the face of the uncertainties it seems best to view this figure in a general way. Paul points to a period of progressive lawlessness in the world prior to the Lord's return. Out of this will emerge a "man of lawlessness" who will personify all anarchy. He will oppose everything relating to God. He will, indeed, set himself up as God—in every sense being *anti-Christ.* But at his return Christ will slay him and his forces by the "breath of his mouth" (2 Thess. 2:8; Rev. 19:20-21). It is thus that Christ will be "KING OF KINGS AND LORD OF LORDS" (Rev. 19:16).

Christian. The term "Christian" is found only three times in the New Testament (Acts 11:26; 26:28; 1 Pet. 4:16). This may seem strange, since it is the most commonly used term today to designate followers of Jesus Christ. But in the New Testament they called themselves by such names as "saints" (1 Cor. 1:1), "disciples" (Acts

1:13), "believers" (Acts 5:14), "servants" or slaves of Christ (Rom. 6:22), "brethren" (Acts 6:3), and "the elect" (Col. 3:12).

The first use of "Christians" to denote Christ's followers is found in Acts 11:26 and gives the origin of the term. It was in Antioch in Syria, a pagan city. It was here for the first time that the gospel was preached to pagans with no previous connection with Judaism. The reading "And it came to pass . . . the disciples were called Christians first in Antioch" shows that they did not so call themselves. Certainly the Jews would not relate them to the name "Christ." They called them "Nazarenes" (Acts 24:5) and those of "this way" (Acts 9:2). Therefore, it may be concluded that it was a name given by pagans to believers in Christ to distinguish them from Jews. These "Christians" were not Jews but Greeks (Acts 11:20).

The Greek word is *Christianos*. This usage of adding *ianos* is found elsewhere. It was used with "Herod" *(Herodianos)* to denote followers of Herod (Matt. 22:16). These were Jews who wished to reestablish a Herod on the throne of Judea. Examples of this usage have been found of *Kaisarianos* or a follower of Caesar. So a "Christian" is a follower of Christ, one who is obedient to him, and who enthrones him in his life.

The second use is in Acts 26:28. The King James Version reads of Agrippa saying to Paul, "Almost thou persuadest me to be a Christian." However, the word rendered "almost" means "in a little." It could refer to time, words, effort, or persuasion. Agrippa was not under conviction. He was bored. So he interrupted Paul's preaching. It may well read, "In short, you are persuading to make me a Christian." He used the term in contempt.

The third example is in 1 Peter 4:16. Peter admonishes his readers that if they suffer at the hands of the Romans it should not be as a lawbreaker, but "as a Christian" or for their loyalty to Christ.

A. T. Robertson notes that the three uses of "Christian" in the New Testament "are from the heathen standpoint" (*Word Pictures in the New Testament* [Nashville: Broadman Press, 1930, Volume III], p. 161). Pagans in Antioch coined it. Agrippa, more pagan than Jewish, scorned it. Peter's use was related to Roman persecution. But through the centuries it has become one of the most cherished and honorable titles. Those who wear this title should follow Christ, be loyal to him, and enthrone him in their lives.

Christianity. The term "Christianity" does not appear in the New Testament. Its origin is usually traced to Ignatius of Antioch (about A.D. 50-117). He used the term "Christianism" (note "Judaism"). Since the term "Christian" was by then an honored one, he exhorted Christians "to live according to Christianism" (Ignatius, *Ad Magnes,* 10). It is of interest to note that both "Christian" (Acts 11:26) and "Christianism" originated in Antioch. The former was coined by pagans to refer to Christ's followers; the latter originated among Christians themselves to refer to their way of life. And as *Judaism* involved the entire system of its laws, rituals, and teachings, so we may see *Christianism* as composing the sum total of the gospel and the person and work of Jesus Christ.

Christianity arose out of the life and work of Jesus Christ. His claim to being "the Christ" was vindicated by his resurrection from the dead (Rom. 1:4). Paul summed up the whole of it in 1 Corinthians 15:3-4 (note verses 5-10; see also 2 Cor. 5:18-21). Christ came into the world as Jesus Christ, the God-Man, the Redeemer of all who believe in him. He died for our sins, and was raised for our justification before God (Rom. 4:25). The body of belief and movement through the centuries to call men to be reconciled to God is what Christianity is all about. But it rests not upon a formulated code of belief. It centers in a Person. Historically Christianity rests on the fact of a Risen Lord.

Church. The English word "church" (note "kirk") is derived from the Greek word *kuriakos,* "of or belonging to the Lord" (Lord, Greek *kurios*). But the word so translated in the New Testament is *ekklēsia* or *ecclesia* (Latin form), the called out ones. While this word appears one hundred and fifteen times in the New Testament it is recorded as used by Jesus only on two occasions (Matt. 16:18; 18:17). The former speaks of the church in the general sense. The latter supposes a local church.

Jesus' former reference to the church was in response to Peter's confession "Thou art the Christ, the Son of the living God" (Matt. 16:16). "Thou art Peter, and upon this rock I will build my church; and the gates of hell [Hades, abode of the dead] shall not prevail [have strength] against it. And I will give unto thee the keys of the kingdom of heaven: and whatsoever thou shalt bind on earth shall be bound in heaven: and whatsoever thou shalt loose on earth shall be loosed in heaven" (Matt. 16:18-19).

Since "art" (v. 16) is singular, Roman Catholics and some others see this verse as addressed to Peter alone. Therefore, they conclude that the church is built upon Peter. However, Jesus' question as to his identity was addressed to the twelve apostles. It may be assumed that, ever ready with an answer, Peter spoke for the group. In this light Jesus' reply may be seen as through Peter to the group. Also "Peter" *(petros)* is masculine gender and "rock" *(petra)* is feminine. So the two cannot refer to the same thing. If it be insisted that Jesus spoke in Aramaic where no such distinction holds, at least one may assume that Matthew wrote in Greek the sense of Jesus' words. In this light it is of interest to note that in the Old Testament whenever "rock" is used in a spiritual sense it refers to deity.

A further distinction may be seen in the meaning of the words for "rock" and "Peter." The former denotes a large stone such as a foundation stone for a building or cliff. One may still see such a rock as the base of a cliff at *Caesarea Philippi* (modern Banias). In 1 Corinthians 3:11 Christ is called the foundation of the church. The word for "Peter" means a smaller stone broken off the larger ledge rock, and partaking of its nature. It is reasonable, therefore, to see Christ as the "rock," and those like Peter who confess Jesus as the Christ as the smaller stones used in building the superstructure. Peter implies as much in 1 Peter 2:5, even though the Greek word for "stones" is a different one.

However, the heart of Jesus' statement is found in "my." The Greek text reads not "the church of me" but "of me the church." Thus "of me" or "my" is emphatic. The sense of this may be seen in the nature of the "church."

The word *ecclesia* was used to refer to the "assembly" (Acts 19:39,41) or "called out ones" in a free city-state (Ephesus was such in the Roman empire) where legal matters were handled in a purely democratic manner. In the Roman empire such must be done within the framework of the empire's laws. So the word was used in the political sense of a local *assembly* operating through democratic processes within the framework of the laws of the Roman empire. In the Septuagint (Greek translation of the Old Testament) this word translates *qahal,* the assembly of Israel (all of God's people) in the wilderness before God and under his direct theocratic rule. It is so used in the New Testament (Acts 7:38). Jesus' disciples would be familiar with both uses of *ecclesia.*

Thus, in effect, Jesus said, "The Greeks and Hebrews have *their* assemblies. Now I will build *my* assembly" or church. As such it partakes of the nature of the others. It is a local assembly of Christians operating through democratic processes under the lordship of Jesus Christ. It is also all of God's redeemed through the ages assembled before him and under his direct theocratic rule. B. H. Carroll once noted that the church in this latter sense would not be in fact until all the redeemed are in heaven. However, the New Testament uses the word "church" a few times in this sense as being true now. J. M. Pendleton in his *Church Manual* says on page 1 that the word is used a few times in the New Testament to refer to the redeemed "in the aggregate."

Ninety-three times the New Testament uses the word to refer to the local church. Even when used in the general sense (cf. Eph. 1:22-23; 3:10-11; Col. 1:18) it is usually in letters written to a local church or, as in Ephesians, to several local churches. What is said here of the church general (also Matt. 16:18) may well also apply to local churches. In the New Testament "church" is never used of a group of churches or of a denomination. Where more than one local church is involved it is always plural (Gal. 1:2; Rev. 1:11, but note the singular form in Revelation 2-3).

The term "autonomy" meaning self-rule should never be used to mean that a local church can do as *it pleases.* Such is anarchy. It should mean as *Christ pleases.* A local church should seek to determine the Lord's will and be governed thereby (1 Cor. 5:1-5). In this light, the decision of the church should evoke the cooperation of all its people. While in the New Testament local churches were independent, they voluntarily cooperated in matters of mutual concern: for instance, doctrinal matters (Acts 15; Gal. 2) and monetary relief of suffering saints (1 Cor. 16:1-4; 2 Cor. 8-9).

The New Testament does not speak of church *membership* but of church *fellowship* (Acts 2:42). The Greek word means sharing or having all things in common, including both privileges and responsibilities. This fellowship is created by the work of the Holy Spirit in the lives of believers (1 Cor. 12:13). One who habitually and deliberately absents himself from the assembly is not in fellowship (Heb. 10:25). If one attends all meetings but is out of harmony with other believers, he is not in fellowship.

Paul likens the church to the human body (1 Cor. 12). As the human body has many members with different functions, so is the body of Christ. Each part must function properly for the good of the whole. The Holy Spirit bestows different gifts upon individual Christians to be used for service and not simply as a source of inordinate pride (1 Cor. 12:4-31). All gifts are to be exercised in the spirit of Christian love (1 Cor. 13). The church as well as the individual Christian is described as the "temple" or Holy of Holies of the Holy Spirit (1 Cor. 3:16; 6:19-20). The Christian's spirit indwells his body. The Spirit indwells his spirit and, thus the body. Indwelling believers, the Spirit also indwells the church fellowship. With Christ as its Head, the church should grow up so that the body will be commensurate to the Head (Eph. 4:11-16).

When Christ said, "The gates of hell [Hades, the abode of the dead] shall not prevail [have strength] against it" (Matt. 16:18), he said that his church will live. Some say the church has no message or ministry to meet the needs of the present day. Thus many well-meaning Christians give their primary loyalty and support to other worthy causes. But when these shall have passed away the church will still be in business for the Lord. For it has the only message and ministry for meeting men's deepest needs.

A literal translation of Matthew 16:19 (see also Matt. 18:18, spoken of a local church) reads, "And I will give unto thee [singular, but spoken through Peter to the group] the keys of the kingdom of heaven: and whatsoever thou shalt bind on earth shall have been bound in heaven: and whatsoever thou shalt loose on earth shall have been loosed in heaven." Keys are for locking or unlocking doors, here the doors into the kingdom of heaven. The writer sees these keys as the gospel which has been committed to the church or churches. If it be bound by not proclaiming it, the doors remain locked. Heaven has already decreed that there is no other way by which men may be saved. If the gospel be loosed upon the earth men will hear it, many will believe, and heaven has already decreed that all who believe the gospel will be saved thereby.

It is a great privilege. And it is an awesome responsibility.

Citizenship. This word is of interest to Christians because of its relation to Paul. The Greek word so translated is one of a family of words based on the word for "city" *(polis)*. The verb means to behave as a citizen. The English word "politics" comes from it.

Though a Jew Paul was a Roman citizen (Acts 22:25). One might become such in one of three ways: (1) by purchase (Acts 22:28a); (2) by rendering some great service to the empire; (3) by birth (Acts 22:28b). Paul was the last of these. In some way Paul's father or even grandfather had become a Roman citizen. Hence Paul was one by birth. As such he enjoyed certain rights, among them being exemption from harsh, shameful punishments such as being beaten with rods or whips; exemption from death by crucifixion (as a Roman subject Jesus was crucified, Paul probably was beheaded by a sword); and the right to appeal to Caesar and to appear personally before him. On more than one occasion Paul availed himself of the first and third rights. His three beatings with rods (2 Cor. 11:25) were evidently administered without knowledge of his citizenship (Acts 16:22,37-39, evidently Silas was also a Roman citizen). But Paul's citizenship saved him from such in Jerusalem (Acts 22:24-29). And despairing of justice in Caesarea, he appealed to Caesar (Acts 25:11-12, 21; 26:32).

Paul drew upon this matter of citizenship to express spiritual truths. In Acts 23:1 "lived" renders the verb "to behave as a citizen." Accused of teaching contrary to Judaism, he avowed that he had always behaved as a good citizen of God's kingdom. The terms "commonwealth" (Eph. 2:12) and "fellow-citizens" (Eph. 2:19) are forms of this word. "Let your conversation be" (Phil. 1:27) renders this verb.

Since Philippi was a Roman colony whose members were Roman citizens (Acts 16:12), Philippians 1:27 reminds the Christians there that they are citizens of a greater kingdom, a heavenly one. "Conversation" (Phil. 3:20, KJV) translates a form of this word. Various translations bring out the idea of heavenly citizenship (cf. American Standard Version, "citizenship"; Henry Alford, "our country is in heaven"; Twentieth Century New Testament, "the State of which we are citizens is in Heaven." Weymouth, "free citizens of Heaven"; Phillips, "citizens of Heaven"). Moffatt renders it, "We are a colony of heaven." This last is most expressive.

Philippi became a full colony by an act of Octavius (Augustus) following his victory at Actium in 31 B.C. It received the same status as Italian cities, including municipal self-government and exemption from poll and land taxes. It was a little bit of Rome set down in the empire, whose citizens should live as Romans for an example to the conquered people. In a sense it was also to protect the interests of the empire.

Thus Paul reminds his Philippian readers that they are a little bit of heaven set down in a hostile, pagan world. Enjoying the privileges of heaven's citizens, they were also to safeguard heaven's interests and so live as to exemplify Christian values. Thus they would encourage others to become Christians. In a very real sense every Christian is a citizen of heaven, every church is a colony of heaven. It is a great privilege. But it also carries a great responsibility.

Comforter. This word translates a Greek word which is Anglicized as "Paraclete." It is found in the New Testament only in John's writings: John 14:16,26; 15:26; 16:7; 1 John 2:1. In the Gospel it refers to the Holy Spirit. In 1 John it is used of Jesus.

Literally, the word means "called to one's side." It was used of a lawyer, especially for the defense, who stood alongside one in court. Since his work includes more than comfort, he may well be called the "Divine Helper." He is truth and guides into all truth (John 14:17; 16:13). He reminds one of Jesus' teachings and enables one to comprehend them (John 14:26). He convicts the world of sin, righteousness, and judgment (John 16:7-11). He does not reveal himself but Christ (John 16:12-13). And his role is to glorify Christ (John 16:14).

First John 2:1 renders this word as "advocate" (KJV), the Latin derivative which is equivalent to the Greek word "one called alongside." So as the Holy Spirit is God's advocate before men's hearts, Jesus Christ is the Christian's advocate before God. See *Holy Spirit, Revelation, Inspiration, Illumination.*

Comfortless. This translates the Greek word *orphanos,* "orphans." Note our word "orphan." This Greek word is found in the New Testament in John 14:18 and James 1:27 where it is rendered "fatherless."

In John 14 Jesus is seeking to prepare his disciples for his death and ascension back into heaven. He upon whom they had depended would be taken from them in bodily presence. But he does not leave them as orphans in the world. Both he and the Father will be with them in abiding presence through the Holy Spirit (John 14:16; see also Matt. 28:20). In the latter reference "alway" renders "all the days" or "every single kind of day": good and bad days; days of joy or sorrow, victory or defeat. What a blessed truth to know that Christians are not orphans in the world!

Confession. The Greek verb "to confess" means "to say the same thing." It is an avowal or acknowledgement of something. In the larger sense confession may be grouped under two headings: confession of sins and confession of faith.

At the human level the New Testament teaches that one should confess to another a wrong done to him (James 5:16; see Luke 17:4). Of course, this implies repentance and a desire for forgiveness from the wronged person. At this point it should be noted that the New Testament does not teach "confession" as practiced in the Roman church. This was a later development.

With respect to God confession may be seen as twofold: confession of sin to God who has been wronged by one's sin; and confession of Christ as one's Savior from sin. In Acts 19:18 the confession of sin is not made to Paul as a *priest*. The confession came as a result of his preaching, but the confession was to God. Indeed, "confessed" here may be seen as an acknowledgement of "their deeds." But the idea of confession to God is involved also. First John 1:9 was written to Christians. But one does not do violence to the idea to apply it as a promise to lost people who confess their sins and turn to Christ.

In the sense of confession of sin, it is related to conviction of sin, repentance from sin, and faith in Christ. If one is convicted of his sin, he may rebel and plunge deeper into sin. But if he repents, he will confess, and believe in Christ. Of course, this involves a change in one's attitudes and conduct (see *Repentance*).

Confession of faith is related to God in Christ. It is an acknowledgement of one's sin and need for a Savior, and it is the fruit of faith in Christ as that Savior. In Matthew 10:32 Jesus said, "Whosoever therefore that shall confess me before men, him will I confess also before my Father which is in heaven." Note that this does not involve *secret discipleship*. "Before men" involves an acknowledgement of Christ as Savior before the fellowship of believers—and a life lived before men which gives evidence of a changed life.

In Hebrews 3:1; 4:14 the Greek word is rendered "profession" (KJV). But the idea is the same. It involves here the entire body of Christian faith and conduct in contrast to that of the Old Testament. Because God's revelation of himself is greater in the New Testament, more is expected of the followers of Christ.

Generally in the New Testament "confess" refers to a willing act on the part of a person. But in Philippians 2:11 it has a dual idea. Read with verse 10 ("heaven . . . earth . . . under the earth") the following idea appears. Certainly those in heaven will "confess that Jesus Christ is Lord." All on earth should do so. "Under the earth" suggests that even those in hell will one day make this confession but with an entirely different sense. They will be forced by the Lord's might to confess or acknowledge that he whom they rejected truly is "Lord" or Jehovah in flesh acting for man's redemption. But, alas, for them it will be everlastingly too late! It is infinitely better to make this willing confession now than to be forced to make it when all hope is gone.

Conscience. The word rendered "conscience" is used in the New Testament thirty-two times. The English word is of Latin origin: *conscientia* which carries the sense of "joint-knowledge," the same meaning as that in the Greek word. The Greek verb form carries not only the idea of joint-knowledge with others but the sense of seeing with one's mind or a knowledge within one's self.

"Let your conscience be your guide" is a proverbial saying. But actually the conscience is the inner voice of God which says in a given situation, "Do right." One's moral judgment tells him what is right. God's revelation through the Bible is necessary for right conduct.

For instance, when Jesus revealed the sins of those who brought to him the woman taken in adultery, they were "convicted by their own conscience" (John 8:9). Paul's conscience told him to do right. And because of his enlightened moral judgment he could say, "I have lived in all good conscience before God until this day" (Acts 23:1; see also Acts 24:16; Rom. 9:1-3). He exhorted men to live right, not out of fear of punishment, "but also for conscience sake" (Rom. 13:5). In 1 Corinthians he dealt with the matter of eating meat offered to idols. Though he held with some that such was not idol worship, others with a weak conscience felt that it was (8:7). Their conscience told them to do right. But their moral judgment told them that eating such meat was wrong. So for their sake Paul would eat no meat (1 Cor. 8:13). However, he also counseled that one who held no such view, when invited to eat with an unbeliever, should not for conscience sake question the place whence the meat came (1 Cor. 10:27). But no Christian should assert his rights, if in doing so he injures the conscience of another. This rule applies in all conduct. To do right is to do nothing that will offend another's conscience.

One vital use of the word "conscience" is found in Romans 2:15. It relates to God's revelation of his will even in the conscience of pagan people. Chrysostom once said that conscience and nature are two books in which the human mind can read of God, previous to supernatural revelation (see Rom. 1:19-20; 2:15). The pagan corrupted the natural revelation into idolatry and every kind of evil (Rom. 1:21-32). But beyond that Paul says that the Jew has God's revelation through the Scriptures, and the pagan in his conscience. It is the responsibility of those with God's written revelation to instruct the moral judgment of the pagan.

In both cases the conscience says, "Do right." But neither does as well as he knows. This is why salvation must be by God's grace and not by man's works.

Conversion. The noun "conversion" appears only one time in the New Testament (Acts 15:3), when Paul and Barnabas declared "the conversion of the Gentiles" from paganism to Christ. But the verb whence it is formed occurs thirty-nine times. It is variously rendered "turn," "be converted," "return," "turn about," and "turn again." This is a compound form of a basic verb which is found eighteen times. It is translated "be converted" only one time (Matt. 18:3) where the sense is to change one's mind or attitude about greatness in the kingdom of heaven. The meaning of this basic verb is to turn. The compound verb mentioned above means to turn around in a religious or moral sense (Luke 1:16)—to turn from something (or one) to something else (or another) (1 Thess. 1:9). When it means to turn around in a moral or religious sense it carries the idea of repentance. The context must determine each case.

When used as in 1 Thessalonians 1:9 the verb carries the thought of repentance and faith resulting in regeneration. Unfortunately, "conversion" is used today in this sense altogether. But that it may have another meaning is seen in Luke 22:32. Predicting Peter's denial of him Jesus said, "But I have prayed for thee, that thy faith fail not: and when thou art converted, strengthen thy brethren." This does not mean that Peter would be lost and need to be saved again. It means that he would recover from his fearful way and turn around from it. He was still a child of God, but needed to repent and turn from his sinful way (see 1 John 1:9). So a *conversion* experience may mean a new experience of dedication on the part of a Christian. A person experiences only one *regeneration.* But he may experience many *conversions.*

Conviction; Convict. The English word "conviction" does not appear in the Bible. The verb "convict" appears only once (John 8:9). But "convince" which translates the same word is used four times (John 8:46; 1 Cor. 14:24; Titus 1:9; James 2:9). Altogether this verb is found in the New Testament seventeen times, and is variously translated besides the above: reprove (Luke 3:19; John 3:20; 16:8; Eph. 5:11,13; 2 Tim. 4:2); rebuke (I Tim. 5:20; Titus 1:13; 2:15; Heb. 12:5); tell one's fault (Matt. 18:15). Moulton and Milligan (*The Vocabulary of the Greek New Testament* [Grand

Rapids, Eerdmans, 1949], p. 202) gives the meaning from the papyri (Greek writings in ordinary life) in 1 Corinthians 14:21; Ephesians 5:11 as "expose."

But the use in the papyri for the most part carries a legal sense. It means through evidence to reveal one's true character and conduct (John 3:20; 8:9,46; 16:8). As would be expected the New Testament uses this word with relation to sin or other wrongdoing. While men may reprove others as in debate or correction (Titus 1:13; 2:15), conviction of sin in the classical sense is the result of the work of the Holy Spirit. By pressing upon one the evidence of his sin, he leads him to render judgment in his own heart that he is a sinner lost from God (Rom. 3:19).

Jesus said that the Holy Spirit would "reprove" or convict the world of sin, righteousness, and judgment. Of sin which he has, of righteousness which he does not possess, and of the judgment he must face before God if he does not repent and believe in Christ.

Conviction is not to be equated with salvation. The convicted person will either repent and believe in Jesus, or he will rebel and plunge deeper into sin. The latter is without excuse before God.

Corban. This is a Hebrew word meaning "a gift" or "that which is brought near" to the altar. Occurring often in the Old Testament, it is found in the New Testament only in Mark 7:11 where it is rendered "Corban" and in Matthew 27:6 as "treasury" where gifts were placed. Mark translates it into Greek as "a gift."

Actually the word could refer to any sacrifice. But in time it gave rise to a most objectionable practice.

A man could dedicate his property to the Temple simply by pronouncing it "Corban." Henceforth, in principle but not necessarily in practice, it belonged to the Temple. The one so doing could retain possession of his property, even in some cases later revoke it. But he could by this custom be justified in not supporting his needy parents. It is no wonder that Jesus used this practice as an example of the utter hypocrisy of many Jewish traditions which were in violation of both the letter and spirit of the Scriptures.

Corinth. Since Corinth figures so greatly in Paul's ministry, a brief word should be written about it. This city was strategically located so as to make it a great commercial center. It had three harbors, Lechaeum on the Corinthian and Cenchreae and Schoenus on the Sardonic Gulf. Thus it commanded the maritime traffic from both east and west. The Mediterranean provided rough sailing in this area. Over the narrow isthmus which connected it with the mainland smaller vessels were transported on a tramway. Cargoes of larger ships were unloaded and taken across to be loaded on other ships. In A.D. 66-67 Nero tried but abandoned an effort to dig a canal across it. In modern times such a canal exists.

Corinth was destroyed by the Roman Mummius in 146 B.C. and was rebuilt by Julius Caesar in 46 B.C., after which it soon regained its commercial supremacy. The city had a pseudo culture but never achieved the heights of Athens in this field. It has been noted that no Corinthian achieved distinction in the literary field.

As a commercial center the city was a polyglot of people, languages, religions, and vices from all over the ancient world. The chief deity of Corinth was Aphrodite, the Greek goddess of sex. Her worship tainted the entire moral climate of the area. At one time one thousand priestesses were used in sex orgies in her temple located on the Acrocorinthus which towered eighteen hundred feet above this city. So low were the morals of Corinth that the worst one could say about a person's moral conduct was to say that he *corinthianized* (note "sodomite" from Sodom).

It was in this city that Paul spent eighteen months during his second missionary journey and three months during his third (Acts 18:11; 20:2-3). It is no wonder that he came to this city "in fear, and in much trembling" (1 Cor. 2:3). The church which he established there caused him more heartache than any other. 1 and 2 Corinthians, written from Ephesus and Macedonia respectively, reflect the conditions in the city itself.

1 and 2 Thessalonians, probably Paul's first epistles, were written from Corinth shortly after his arrival on his first visit to the city (1 Thess. 3:6). It was during his second visit to this city that he wrote Romans and probably Galatians. (See Acts 20:3b; Rom. 15:24-27; 1 Cor. 16:3-4).

Corinthian Epistles. While the purpose of this work does not include an exhaustive study of New Testament books, it is well to note that these epistles belong to "the Big Four" (1 and 2 Corinthians, Galatians, and Romans). In the nineteenth-century storm of criticism which raged about the epistles of Paul, only these four won virtually unanimous agreement as to their Pauline authorship. (This restricted view has not prevailed in the twentieth century.)

Cornelius. A Roman centurion (commander of one hundred soldiers) stationed in Caesarea, he was the first Gentile (neither a Jew nor a Jewish proselyte, a Gentile who had adopted the Jewish faith) to whom the gospel was preached (Acts 10). "One that feared God" probably means that he was a "God-fearer" (Acts 10:2). Such were Gentiles who were studying Judaism but who had not formally and ceremonially adopted it as their faith. Of interest is the fact that in the sixteen New Testament references to centurions they always appear as good men.

Cornerstone. The word "cornerstone" or its equivalent appears often in the Old Testament. Two suggested meanings of this stone are (1) the foundation-stone upon which a building rested (Job 38:6; Isa. 28:16; Jer. 51:26); (2) the capstone which finished the structure, possibly the center stone of an arch which held other stones in place (Psalm 118:22; Zech. 4:7). In either case it was used figuratively of the Messiah. In Zechariah 10:4 it connotes the ruler in the Messianic age.

Jesus quoted Psalm 118:22 with reference to himself as its fulfilment (Matt. 21:42; Mark 12:10; Luke 20:17; see also Peter in Acts 4:11; 1 Pet 2:7, and Paul in Eph. 2:20). Note the combination of ideas of the foundation stone and capstone in Matthew 21:44. On Isaiah 28:16 see Romans 9:33; 1 Peter 2:6. All of these Old Testament passages were considered by the rabbis as Messianic, which adds to their significance in the New Testament. Christ is the cornerstone/capstone in God's redemptive structure. One should be careful not to reject his Chosen One.

Covenant. The idea of a covenant appears often in the Old Testament. When used of men it carries the idea of a contract binding upon both parties. However, then as now, a greater party might impose conditions which must be kept by the lesser party before the greater was bound by it.

The two principal covenants between God and men are the ones made with Abraham (Gen. 12:1-3) and with Israel (Exod. 19:1-8). The former is an unconditional covenant of grace; the latter is a conditional covenant of law and service (note "if" and "then," Exod. 19:5). Until Israel kept the "if" Jehovah was not bound by the "then" (Matt. 21:33-45; 1 Pet. 2:1-10, note how Peter combines the language of the passages in Exodus 19:5-6 and Matthew 21:42-44). Covenants were sealed in blood (Exod. 24:3-8). The author of Hebrews sees the Abrahamic covenant as sealed in the blood of Christ (9:11-26). The New Covenant of Hebrews 8:1 to 9:26 is in fulfilment of Jeremiah 31:31-34 which foresees the removal of the old Mosaic covenant. But the covenant of grace made with Abraham centers in Christ (Gen. 15:5; Gal. 3:16), and is therefore an everlasting covenant (Heb. 13:20; see Matt. 26:28).

Covetousness. One of the Ten Commandments says, "Thou shalt not covet thy neighbour's house . . . wife . . . manservant . . . maidservant . . . ox . . . ass, nor any thing that is thy neighbour's" (Exod. 20:17). Thus it is forbidden along with murder, adultery, theft, and idolatry. Jesus said, "Beware of covetousness" (Luke 12:15). Paul called covetousness "idolatry" (Col. 3:5). The Greek word so translated means "the desire for more," inordinate, of course. This desire may relate to money, sex, or any other physical appetite.

It is listed as one of the worst of sins (1 Cor. 6:10; Eph. 5:3; 1 Tim. 6:9-10.) It is not money, but "the love of money" which is the root of every kind of evil (1 Tim. 6:10; see also Acts 5:1-10). It was covetousness which led Judas to betray Jesus (Matt. 26:14-15). Covetousness is the root out of which grows lying, murder, illicit sex, rape, drunkenness, war—indeed, every foolish and harmful lust (1 Tim. 6:9). If one will keep this sin out of his heart, he will keep it out of every other expression of his body.

Creation. Apart from divine revelation there is no ultimate explanation of the origin of the universe. Human reason with futility moves back from *effect* to *cause*. But eventually it reaches the place where there is no natural *cause*. Not even the theory of the eternity of matter provides the answer. For even this leaves a gap which neither human reason nor natural phenomena can bridge. There comes the place where men must make the leap of faith. This the Bible does when it says, "In the beginning God created the heaven and the earth" (Gen. 1:1).

The Bible is not primarily concerned with the *how* but the *Who* in creation. Science, which is limited to phenomena, may explore the *how* and *what,* but only faith or religion can declare the *Who.* There may be conflict between some scientists and some theologians. But true science and true theology do not conflict. They both are of God, who does not contradict himself. "In the beginning" is flexible enough to fit any *proved* evidence of science as to the time span of creation. The word rendered "day" in Genesis 1, like the English word, is used to specify various lengths of time or events in history. And in the broader sense the creative order in Genesis 1 corresponds to the conclusions of science which admits to a creative, purposeful process for the natural order.

The Bible clearly teaches that the triune God is the Creator (Gen. 1:1-2; John 1:3; Col. 1:16; Heb. 1:1-2). Thus creation is not out of nothing. It is the expression of God's infinite love and power. Literally, "For out of [as source] him, and through [as agent] him, and unto [as goal] him is the universe as a whole" (Rom. 11:36).

John, Paul, and the author of Hebrews all point to Christ as the intermediate Agent in the creative work. A literal rendering of John 1:3 reads, "Every single part of the universe through him [Christ] came into being, and apart from him came into being not even one thing which has come into being." He created the universe—from atoms to solar systems. Likewise, Colossians 1:16. "Because *in* him alone was created the universe as a whole . . . and the universe as a whole *through* him and *unto* him stands created." The italicized words show him to be the *sphere* in which creation took place, the *intermediate agent* in creation, and the *goal* toward which it moves. Furthermore, Colossians 1:17 reads, "And he himself is before every single part of the universe, and the universe as a whole in him holds together." The universe is neither geocentric nor heliocentric, earth- or sun-centered. It is Christocentric or Christ-centered. The universe is not sun-centered but Son-centered. The more we learn of the universe the greater is our understanding of the glory of Christ.

Paul sees the goal of history to be a redeemed natural and spiritual universe presented by the Son to the Father, "that God [Father, Son, Spirit] may be all in all" (1 Cor. 15:27-28).

Cross; Crucifixion. The cross, an instrument of excruciating suffering and shame, is the most glorious symbol of the Christian faith. For it was on such that Jesus died to redeem a lost world.

Crucifixion was probably invented by the Phoenicians and produced the most agonizing of deaths. According to ancient historians this method of execution was used by Egyptians, Persians, Babylonians, Greeks, and Romans. In the interbiblical period it was even used by some Jewish rulers. But as a whole it was abhorred by the Jews (Gal. 3:13; see Deut. 21:23). It was forbidden to crucify a Roman citizen (Cicero, *Pro Rabirio 5*). This method was used only for the worst of criminals.

Among the Romans crucifixion was preceded by scourging (Matt. 27:26). The victim bore his own cross to the place of crucifixion. Due to his previous ordeal Jesus fell under the weight of his cross which was then borne by another (Luke 23:26; John 19:17). Victims were crucified naked (John 19:23-24). According to custom one end of the upright pole of the cross was placed in a hole in the ground. The cross piece was laid on the ground. Jesus was made to lie on the ground. To render him helpless his legs and arms were jerked out of place. With his arms stretched out on the crossbeam, his hands were nailed to it. Lifting his body into place the soldiers fastened the beam to the pole. His feet rested on a little shelf about two feet above the ground, crossed, and nailed to the pole with a spike. He was left hanging there until he died.

The suffering was intense. Due to loss of blood and the sun, one of the greatest agonies was thirst. The body became fevered, lips parched, the throat inflamed, the tongue swollen, the voice raspy, and the mind clouded. Even the slightest movement aggravated the nail wounds. Fever and a surcharge of blood to the brain produced a terrific headache. In this strained position the body protruded so that the rib bones might be counted. Blood collecting in the abdomen caused agonizing pain. All this was endured amid the taunting cries of the mob about the cross. The victims of crucifixion literally died a thousand deaths.

Usually it took hours, even days for one to die. Jesus died after six hours (9:00 A.M. to 3:00 P.M., Luke 23:44-46). The terrific ordeal through which he passed prior to the cross took its toll, giving him an early merciful death (John 19:32-37). Some physicians have interpreted the mingling of blood and water (John 19:34) as evidence that Jesus' heart ruptured. Truly he died of a broken heart—for you and me! See Psalm 22 and Isaiah 53.

Cup of the Lord. Three *cups* are mentioned by Jesus with reference to his redemptive work. These are to be understood figuratively with regard to their contents. The first is the cup of his sufferings (Matt. 20:22-23; Mark 10:38-39). The second is the cup used at the Last Supper symbolizing his blood shed for man's sin. "This cup is the new testament [covenant] in my blood, which is shed for you" (Luke 22:20; 1 Cor. 11:25). Paul called it "the cup of the Lord" (1 Cor. 10:21; see also 1 Cor. 10:16).

The third is the cup which in Gethsemane he prayed to be spared (Matt. 26:39; Mark 14:36; Luke 22:42). To the Father he prayed, "If thou be willing, remove this cup from me: nevertheless not my will, but thine, be done" (Luke 22:42).

What does this cup represent? That he might be spared physical death? Hardly. He had repeatedly referred to it. Multitudes have gladly died for him; he was no less brave than they. That he would not die in Gethsemane? See Luke 22:44. He knew he would die on a cross. That God would raise him after death? Again, he had often predicted his resurrection on the third day (Matt. 16:21; Luke 18:31-33; John 2:19, 21-22). The writer sees this cup, not as physical death, but what it entailed—his becoming sin for man's sin (2 Cor. 5:21). All the sin of the world was reduced to one cup of nauseous brew which he was to drink. And his sensitive, sinless spirit drew back from it in horror. But since there was no other way to save men, he drank it. He who knew no sin was made, not sinful, but sin for lost men.

Damnation; Condemnation. In modern English these words are related to eternal loss in hell. But in the New Testament this may or may not be true. The context must decide.

For instance, in 2 Peter 2:3 the word rendered "damnation" means "destruction." In 2:1 it is rendered both "damnable" and "destruction." False prophets who seek to destroy others will themselves be destroyed. The context calls for destruction in hell. This Greek word is used sixteen other times in the New Testament. In Matthew 26:8 it refers to waste of substance (Mark 14:4). Otherwise the predominant use is of "perdition" "destruction" (Matt. 7:13; John 17:12 of Judas; Rom. 9:22; Phil. 1:28; 3:19; 2 Thess. 2:3; 1 Tim. 6:9; Heb. 10:39; 2 Pet. 3:7,16; Rev. 17:8,11).

The other uses of "damnation" or "damned" and "condemnation" render words derived from the verb "to judge" (2 Thess. 2:12). In Luke 7:43 it refers to forming an opinion between two alternatives. In John 3:17-18 (condemn) it means to judge. The idea of condemnation must be inferred from the context.

Another compound verb means to judge down. It means to judge and find guilty (see "damned" in Rom. 14:23). This verb seventeen times is translated "condemn" (Matt. 12:41-42; 20:18; 27:3; Mark 10:33; 14:64; Luke 11:31-32; John 8:10-11; Rom. 2:1; 8:3,34; 1 Cor. 11:32; Heb. 11:7; James 5:9; 2 Pet. 2:6). The context in each case makes the sense plain.

Another derivative of the basic verb to judge is rendered "damnation" in Matthew 23:33 where the sense is clearly eternal punishment (see also Mark 3:29; John 5:29). This word is translated "judgment" or the act of judging forty-one times. In Matthew 5:21 it refers to a court judgment. But see also verse 22. Still another word refers to the result of judgment (Matt. 7:2; John 9:39; Acts 24:25; Rom. 2:2-3; 5:16; 11:33; Gal. 5:10; Heb. 6:2; 1 Pet. 4:17; 2 Pet. 2:3; Rev. 17:1; 20:4). This word is rendered "damnation" in Matthew 23:14; Mark 12:40; Luke 20:47; Romans 3:8; 13:2; 1 Corinthians 11:29; 1 Timothy 5:12. In the papyri this word is always found in the sense of one being guilty. All other uses of the word "judgment" mean the act of judging.

The context in each case determines whether the judgment is of God or by men. It also shows whether it is a temporal or an eternal judgment.

Darkness and Light. When used in the figurative sense these words connote evil and good respectively. "Darkness" is used of moral evil (John 3:19; Rom. 13:12). "Outer darkness" refers to the place of punishment. In 1 John 2:11 the meaning is human ignorance produced by a wrong relation to God. "Light," of course, is the opposite of "darkness."

Darkly. This word translates a phrase which means "in a riddle." It appears in the New Testament only in 1 Corinthians 13:12. The word rendered "riddle" has been Anglicized as "enigma." The English version reads, "For now we see through a glass darkly; but then face to face: now I know in part; but then shall I know even as also I am known." Literally, "fully know even as also I am fully known."

The ancients had no glass mirrors, but used polished metal which reflected a blurred image. Paul says that with his fleshly eyes he sees God and/or spiritual things only partially or in a blurred fashion. But in heaven he shall see the Lord face to face. And he will fully know spiritual things clearly, even as he is fully known by the Lord. Earth's knowledge at best is only *out of parts*. It is a poor reflection of complete truth. But in heaven all infirmities will be removed, enabling one to see clearly truth as a whole.

Day. An understanding of the various uses of this word helps in interpreting various passages of Scripture. Like the English word, the Hebrew and Greek words had several uses.

Of course, at times this word refers to twenty-four hours (Lev. 23:27-32; see also Exod. 12:15-20; 2 Cor. 11:25). It was also used to connote the period from sunrise to sunset (Gen. 1:5; 8:22). Also time (Gen. 2:4; 1 Sam. 3:1; Isa. 2:12); some signal event in history (Phil. 1:6); a time of opportunity (John 9:4); and the return of the Lord (Rom. 13:11-12).

From these brief examples one can see that "day" must not always refer to a period of twenty-four hours. This is especially significant as one considers the days of creation in the light of science. One cannot be dogmatic. Whether one sees six twenty-four hour days or indefinite periods of time is a matter of choice. It is not how long God *needed* but how much time he *chose*. He could have created the universe and all in it in a fraction of a second. However, his resting from his creative work on the seventh day lends aid to the idea of indefinite time periods. He is still *resting* from creative work insofar as matter is concerned.

Of interest is the Jewish and Roman methods of determining the hours of the day. In Jesus' day the Jewish daytime began with 6:00 A.M. as the first hour (Mark 15:25,33; "third hour" was 9:00 A.M., "sixth hour" was noon, "ninth hour" was 3:00 P.M.). The Romans counted time from midnight. Some see a conflict between Mark and John 19:14, "sixth hour." This was the time when Pilate sentenced Jesus to death. Most likely John used Jewish time throughout his Gospel except here. In this instance he used the *official* Roman time when Jesus was sentenced to death or at 6:00 A.M. Mark records the hour when the crucifixion began. So there need be no conflict.

The Romans divided the night by the four changes of the guard: "even . . . midnight . . . cockcrowing . . . morning" (Mark 13:35). See also Matthew 14:25; Acts 12:4.

Day of Atonement. See *Atonement, Day of.*

Day of the Lord. See *Eschatology.*

Deacon. The word translated "deacon" renders a Greek word meaning "through dust," probably a slave raising dust in his haste to serve. It connotes the lowest work of a slave. He was the one who rinsed dust from the feet of arriving guests. Both the noun and verb forms are used in Matthew 20:26,28 as "minister" and "ministered." In verse 28 Jesus referred to himself. Note Jesus rinsing his disciples' feet (John 13:4-15). Paul also used this term of himself and Apollos (1 Cor. 3:5).

While the word "deacon" is not used, the origin of the office is probably found in Acts 6:1-7. Philippians is addressed to the "bishops and deacons" of that church. The qualifications of a deacon are found in 1 Timothy 3:8-13. Note the close similarity between these and those of bishops or pastors (1 Tim. 3:1-7). Pastors and deacons are the only ordained church officers mentioned in the New Testament.

The feminine form of the word "deacon" is used of Phoebe in Romans 16:1, where it is translated "servant." From this some see the New Testament supporting the office of "deaconess." Since Paul makes no mention of such in Philippians 1:1 or in 1 Timothy

3, this is open to question. Phoebe may have been simply a woman serving in certain capacities such as ministering to the needy and sick as well as furnishing food and lodging to traveling Christians. One cannot be dogmatic either way.

Death. God made man to live forever. But his rebellion against God made him subject to aging, disease, pain, and death. That this penalty involved physical death is evident from Genesis 2:17; 3:22. However, Adam lived for hundreds of years after this event (Gen. 5:5). "The day that thou eateth thereof thou shalt surely die," therefore, must be seen as indicating spiritual death. The moment man ate the forbidden fruit, he died spiritually. When the spirit is separated from the body, the body is dead (Gen. 3:19). When the spirit is separated from God, the Bible calls this spiritual death. One may be alive in body yet be dead in spirit (Eph. 2:1). Physical death is called an "enemy," yet God causes even this enemy to serve man in releasing him from a body no longer fit for habitation (2 Cor. 5:1). For the Christian this ushers him into an eternal habitation. The old tabernacle or tent is struck down, and the spirit receives "a building of God, an house not made with hands, eternal in the heavens."

The emphasis in the New Testament is placed more strongly upon spiritual death or the spirit's separation from God. Jesus came to remove that separation from all who believe in him (Eph. 2:5-6). In his resurrection he conquered death, both physical and spiritual. Eventually he will destroy death itself (1 Cor. 15:26,54b-57).

At the moment of physical death both the saved and unsaved enter Hades, the abode of the dead (Luke 16:22-23). It is clear, however, that the saved go to heaven (Abraham's bosom was a Jewish concept of heaven) and the lost enter hell as seen in the rich man being "in torments . . . in this flame" (Luke 16:23-24). Unfortunately, in verse 23 "hades" is rendered "hell." This is true throughout the New Testament (KJV) except for 1 Corinthians 15:55 where it is rendered "grave" (see Matt. 11:23; 16:18; Luke 10:15; 16:23; Acts 2:27,31; Rev. 1:18; 6:8; 20:13-14). Both Lazarus and the rich man entered Hades, which simply means that they died. But their conditions were the opposite of what they had known in earthly life. When the Lord returns those who died believing in him will he bring with him (1 Thess. 4:14). This means that they are with him now. The New Testament does not teach "soul sleeping" or an unconscious state between death and the Lord's return. "Sleep" is used as a synonym for death as a cessation of labor, sorrow, and trouble.

Jesus taught the final resurrection of the saved and lost (John 5:28-29). For the former it will be a "resurrection of life"; for the latter a "resurrection of damnation" or judgment. The latter will be "cast into the lake of fire" (Rev. 20:15). This is described as "the second death" (v. 14) or eternal separation from God. See *Gehenna* and *Hell*.

Dedication, Feast of. This feast commemorated the dedication of the temple by Judas Maccabaeus after the desecration by Antiochus Epiphanes who ruled in Antioch 175-164 B.C. This dedication followed his defeat by the Jews under Judas Maccabaeus. It was a feast of joy and gladness, lasting eight days beginning on the 25th day of Kislev (December).

It was at this feast in A.D. 29 that Jesus delivered his message recorded in John 10:22-39. Though not one of the more important feasts, Jesus attended it since he was near Jerusalem at the time.

Demons; Demon Possession. In the New Testament two words are used for "demon," usually rendered "devil" or "devils." *Daimonion,* used sixty times, is rendered "devil" except in Acts 17:18 where it is translated "gods." *Daimōn,* used five times, is rendered "devils," except as "devil" in Luke 8:29. The term "unclean spirit" is also used to denote such beings.

Many ancient peoples had extreme and elaborate systems concerning demons, their appearance, activities, and exorcism. By contrast the New Testament is restrained in treating such. Some interpreters attribute New Testament demonology to ancient superstition, holding that either Jesus shared it or else adapted his language to the beliefs of his contemporaries. Such a position is unworthy of Jesus and ignores the facts. Luke, a physician-scientist, treats demons and demon possession as true to facts (Luke 8:26-36).

The New Testament regards demons as minions of Satan (Matt. 12:22-29; 25:41). Little detail as such is given regarding them. Jesus said that they pass through "dry places, seeking rest, and [find] none" (Matt. 12:43). They are pictured as spiritual beings which long to inhabit some person or animal (Matt. 12:43-45; Mark 5:10-13). Their ultimate place of confinement is the "deep," abyss (Luke 8:31) or bottomless pit.

Demons belong to the spirit world. Their only manifestation is in the disorders they cause. They possessed knowledge of Jesus' true nature (Mark 1:24), yet did not believe in him in the sense of commitment to him (James 2:19). They had the power of speech, but evidently through their victims (Mark 1:23-25,34; Luke 4:41; 8:28). Jesus forbade them to speak of him, for he did not want the testimony of demons. His power over demons shows his superiority over demonic or evil powers (Mark 1:27). He cast out demons by commanding them, not through some elaborate system of exorcism.

Some see certain forms of demon possession as conditions described today in medical terms. However, many cases distinguish between this and disease (Matt. 4:24; 8:16; 10:8; Mark 1:32,34; 6:13; Luke 4:40-41; 9:1; 13:32; Acts 19:12). Not all cases were related to mental or nervous conditions (Matt. 9:32-33; 12:22). Mental conditions are found in Matthew 8:28; Acts 19:13-14. One case was epileptic (Matt. 17:15), but Matthew 4:24 distinguishes between demon possession and epileptic and lunatic diseases.

Nonbiblical literature of the time shows an unusual outbreak of demon possession about the time of Jesus. This suggests that as God came in flesh, Satan's minions countered by indwelling people. These phenomena are but an earthly part of the cosmic struggle between God and Satan. We know far too little about spiritual phenomena to deny that this is the case. Jesus Christ was manifested to destroy the works of the devil (1 John 3:8). Christians today need to take to heart Paul's words that their real enemy is not flesh and blood but evil spiritual powers (Eph. 6:12). See *Satan; Devil.*

Devil. See *Satan.*

Diana; Artemis. Diana is the Latin equivalent of the Greek *Artemis* as the Greek text reads in Acts 19. She was the mother goddess of the earth, said to be the source of all life. This deity was worshiped among other peoples under different names: for instance, Phoenicians (Astarte); Babylonians (Ishtar). Her principal shrine was at Ephesus, where her image was said to have fallen from the sky (Acts 19:35). This image shows her torso covered by what were once thought to be many breasts; they are now seen as eggs symbolizing the origin of life. So rich were the offerings brought to her that her Ephesian shrine was something like a bank today.

A large guild in Ephesus made small shrines of her (Acts 19:24-25). They were made of silver, clay, stone, and wood. Clay and stone ones have been found among the ruins of Ephesus. Silver ones probably were melted down for the metal. So effective was Paul's ministry there that their sale was falling off. So under the leadership of Demetrius a riot started. This resulted in Paul leaving the city ahead of schedule (Acts 19:26 to 20:1).

Discerning of Spirits. This phrase refers to one of the gifts of the Holy Spirit (1 Cor. 12:10; see also Rom. 14:1, "doubtful"; Heb. 5:14, "discern" rendering the Greek word for "discerning"). The word means to judge through or to determine whether one acted, especially teaching or speaking, by the Holy Spirit or the evil spirit.

Disciple; Discipline. The former word simply means "pupil" or "learner." Usually, but not always, it refers to Jesus' followers. It also refers to the pupils of John the Baptist (Matt. 9:14; John 3:25). In John 6:66 "disciples" were those taught by Jesus but who had not fully received him as Savior or the Christ. The context must decide in each case.

The word rendered "discipline" refers to the rearing of a child. It is variously rendered: chastening (Heb. 12:5,7,11), nurture (Eph. 6:4); instruction (2 Tim. 3:16); chastisement (Heb. 12:8). The verb form is likewise translated as "chasten" (1 Cor. 11:32; 2 Cor. 6:9; Heb. 12:6,7,10; Rev. 3:19); "chastise" (Luke 23:16,22); "learn" (Acts 7:22; 1 Tim. 1:20); "teach" (Acts 22:3; Titus 2:12); "instruct" (2 Tim. 2:25).

Divorce. Jesus is recorded as teaching concerning divorce, which implies remarriage, in Mark 10:2-12; Luke 16:18. But his most complete treatment is found in Matthew (5:27-32; 19:3-12). Matthew 5:32 coincides with 19:3-12.

The occasion was a test case brought to Jesus by some Pharisees. Hillel taught divorce for any cause; Shammai only for sexual infidelity. Note that the case involved a man divorcing his wife; it was most difficult for a wife to divorce her husband. The Pharisees sought to trick Jesus on the question of hard or easy divorce. Jesus reaffirmed God's original intent in marriage (Gen. 2:24; Matt. 19:4-6). As for Moses authorizing a "bill of divorcement" (Deut. 24:1-4), he said it was due to the hardness of men's hearts (Matt. 19:7-8). Actually it was an improvement upon current practice. Instead of simply sending his wife away, a man was required to give her evidence in writing that she was divorced so that she might remarry. But Jesus brushed this aside.

He said that "except it be for fornication," divorce could not be granted (Matt. 19:9). Some insist that the exception clause is not genuine. But the manuscript evidence for it is strong. See also Matthew 5:32. Others insist that it is not genuine because Mark's account omits it. But Mark 10:10-12 came later "in the house." The issue with the Pharisees involved a *cause*. The writer holds that the exception clauses in Matthew 5:32 and 19:9 are genuine teachings of Jesus.

A person can be "one flesh" sexually with only one person (1 Cor. 6:16). To become one flesh with another than one's marriage mate breaks that oneness. The injured party may forgive and reestablish that oneness (see Hosea), or may consider the guilty party as though dead. Clearly Jesus taught one and only one ground for divorce and remarriage.

Doubt. Two Greek words are used in the sense of doubt. One means to doubt, be perplexed (Luke 9:7; 24:4; John 13:22; Acts 2:12; 5:24; 10:17; 25:20; 2 Cor. 4:8; Gal. 4:20). The other, meaning to judge between or through, is rendered "doubt" five times (Matt. 21:21; Mark 11:23; Acts 10:20; 11:12; Rom. 14:23).

Any thinking person will at times have doubts; he must judge between two alternatives and at times will be perplexed as to which to choose. In truth doubt is a protective quality given of God. If one says drinking poison will not harm, he should be doubted. If you say that Jesus is not God's virgin-born Son, I will doubt you. But Satan seeks to pervert doubt into unbelief. One should not permit doubt to fester, but, starting with what he knows is true, he should *judge through* to a positive conclusion.

Thomas is an ideal example of this (John 20:24-28). He *knew* of Jesus' crucifixion wounds, and insisted that the resurrection body should bear evidence of them. Finding it so, he confessed, "My Lord and my God." According to the Gospels he is the only one who called Jesus "God." He went through his doubt to a superb faith—from "Doubting Thomas" to "Thomas the Confessor."

Charles Kingsley once said that one should not fear doubt if he has a disposition to believe.

Easter. This word occurs in the King James Version only in Acts 12:4 where it translates the word for "passover" (see 1 Cor. 5:7). There is no evidence of an Easter observance in the New Testament. The early Christians continued to observe the Passover, regarding Christ as the true paschal lamb. Actually they commemorated the Lord's resurrection every first day of the week. "Lord's day" referred to this day (Rev. 1:10).

The observance of Easter was a gradual development attended by much controversy as to the observance itself and how to determine the date. The Council of Nicea in A.D. 325 decreed that it should be observed on Sunday, but did not specify the Sunday. The Western church (Roman Catholic) follows the Gregorian calendar, which, according to its reckoning, means that the day may fall on a given Sunday from March 22 to April 25. It follows the pattern for dating the Passover. The Eastern or Greek church does not follow the Gregorian calendar, which means that the day may fall as much later as five weeks. The latest date is April 30. Through gradual acceptance the Easter commemoration has come to be regarded as the greatest in the Christian church, since it celebrates the most important event of the Christian faith—the resurrection of Christ. See *Lord's Day.*

Elder, Bishop, Pastor. In the Old Testament the title "elder" was basically related to age. By virtue of age and experience one was qualified to give counsel and to rule. In the New Testament the title is found among Jews and is usually associated with scribes and Pharisees. In the early church it was used to denote leaders in the churches (Acts 14:23). Sixty-four out of sixty-six times used in the New Testament the word refers to either Jewish or Christian elders. In the Christian sense it apparently bears the traditional connotation of counsellor.

"Bishop" translates a word which means basically "overseer." The Latin equivalent is "supervisor." It is so translated one time in Acts 20:28. Four times it is rendered "bishop" (Phil. 1:1; 1 Tim. 3:2; Titus 1:7; 1 Pet. 2:25). In secular Greek usage it denoted one overseeing the work of others.

"Pastor" (Eph. 4:11) renders a word meaning "shepherd." The verb means to feed as a shepherd (John 21:16). It is often used of Jesus (John 10:11,12,14; Heb. 13:20). In 1 Peter 2:25 he is called "the Shepherd and Bishop of your souls." In Acts 20:28 the idea of elder, bishop, and pastor or shepherd refers to one office. Paul was speaking to the elders of the church in Ephesus (Acts 20:17). He said, "Take heed therefore unto yourselves, and to all the flock, over which the Holy Ghost [Spirit] hath made you overseers [bishops], to feed [as a shepherd] the church of God." It is generally agreed that in the New Testament these three titles refer to the same office which is summed up today as "pastor." But some Christian groups use "elder" and "bishop" to connote other positions of leadership in the churches.

Election, Doctrine of. Jesus used the word "elect" to refer to Christians (Matt. 24:20,24; see also Romans 16:13, "chosen"). The verb form means to select or choose. From it comes the word "election."

The doctrine of election refers to God's act in choosing those who are saved. Some, placing their emphasis upon God's sovereignty, see this to mean that arbitrarily he has elected certain ones to be saved to the exclusion of all others. However, the missionary commissions of Jesus plus the universal nature of the many invitations to receive Christ seem to point to another meaning. For this position ignores man's free will (Matt. 11:28-30; 28:18-20; John 3:16-18; Acts 1:8; Rom. 10:9-13; Rev. 22:17). Election is not a rigged program. It expresses God's purpose to save, not a few, but as many as he can. It is never presented as contrary to man's free will.

Ephesians is Paul's great treatment of election. In it he shows that God has elected a plan of salvation and a people to propagate that plan. In his sovereignty God has elected. But man is free to accept or reject; he is responsible for his choice.

"Hath chosen" expresses God's purpose (Eph. 1:4). "In love having predestinated" denotes the method in election. The Greek word means to set a boundary beforehand—before the foundation of the world (v. 5). The boundary is Christ, like building a fence about an area. To be inside the fence is to be "in Christ." Ten times in eleven verses (vv. 3-13) the phrase "in Christ" or its equivalent occurs. So in his sovereignty God says that all who are in Christ shall be saved. All outside Christ shall be lost. In his free will (v. 13, "believed") man can decide to be inside or outside the fence. The fact that God knows beforehand who will receive or reject Christ does not mean that he arbitrarily causes it.

It is difficult to improve on an old Negro preacher's explanation of election with respect to salvation. God voted for you. The devil voted against you. It is a tie vote. And you must cast the deciding vote.

The elected people to propagate this plan is the church (Eph. 3:10-11; 1 Pet. 2:1-10). To prepare the church for its mission Christ has given to it "apostles . . . prophets . . . evangelists . . . pastors and teachers" (Eph. 4:11). Apostles were pioneers in planting the gospel, like missionaries. Prophets were those gifted with power in preaching the gospel, like evangelists. Evangelists seem to have been those who worked with churches in a given area (Timothy, 2 Tim. 4:5), like district missionaries. Pastors and teachers refer to one office, those connected with a local church.

The original Greek text had no punctuation marks except the question mark (;). So Ephesians 4:12 does not set forth the duties of the above people. It should read "For the perfecting [equipping] of the saints for the work of the ministry for the edifying [building up] of the body of Christ." They are not to work *for* but *with* the saints in carrying out this phase of God's election.

Emperor Worship. While no such phrase is found in the New Testament, the pagan practice of worshiping the Roman emperors is reflected strongly in certain portions of it, especially in Revelation.

The root of emperor worship was the deification of Rome into a goddess called *Dea Roma.* By building temples to her, conquered peoples showed their loyalty to Rome. Since the emperor personified the empire, it was a simple matter to begin emperor worship.

Julius Caesar, claiming to be divine, had his image placed in temples with the gods. An inscription in the temple in Ephesus read, "To the goddess Roma and the divine Julius." Augustus (27 B.C.-A.D. 14) did not insist upon veneration in Rome, but accepted the title "Sebaste" which means worthy of worship. He did encourage emperor worship in the provinces. Caligula (A.D. 37-41) demanded worship. He was prevented from placing his statue in the Jerusalem temple only by an uproar by the Jews. By the time of Nero (A.D. 54-68) emperor worship was in full swing. Domitian (A.D. 81-96) demanded worship, even refusing to accept correspondence not addressed to him in divine terms. The persecution of Christians reflected in Revelation was due to their refusal to worship his image.

Those worshiping the emperor were required to say, "Lord Caesar." Instead the Christians said, "Lord Jesus." The term "Lord's Day" (Rev. 1:10) probably was in opposition to the observance of days called "Caesar's Day." The confession "Lord Jesus" (Rom. 10:9) and "Jesus Christ is Lord" (Phil. 2:11) probably reflect Christian opposition to saying "Lord Caesar" or "Caesar is Lord." To "confess with thy mouth the Lord Jesus" (Rom. 10:9) may seem rather mild today. But in the first century it could have meant the loss of one's life. But even today such a confession demands all of one's life. See *Lord's Day.*

Eschatology. This word means the doctrine of last things. It relates to the various elements or events concerning the return of Christ and the end of the age. Widely varying views exist around this doctrine—ranging all the way from intricate systems of events to the simple hope and expectation of the Lord's return and the final resurrection and judgment. But all such share in "that blessed hope, and the glorious appearing of the great God and [even] our Saviour Jesus Christ" (Titus 2:13). Among most Christians one's position on the details in eschatology has never been a test of orthodoxy.

Some theologians speak of *realized* and *unrealized* eschatology. The former refers to the first coming of Christ and his Kingdom in men's hearts (Matt. 3:2; 4:17; Luke 17:20-21). In this sense "eternal life" is the quality of life the Christian now has and which extends into eternity (John 3:16; 5:24; 11:25; 14:6). The latter refers to events yet to come at the end of the age.

While Jesus interspersed his teachings with eschatological language, his greatest teaching about it is found in Matthew 24-25 (see parallels in Mark 13; Luke 21:5-36). It should be noted, however, that Jesus was answering three questions: the fall of Jerusalem; the second coming; the end of the age (Matt. 24:3). A careful analysis enables one to distinguish which is involved in given places. Jesus begins by warning against false signs of his return (Matt. 24:4-8). Verses 9-13 seem to refer to the interval up to the fall of Jerusalem. Verse 14 is the most definite sign that Jesus gave as to his coming. Verses 15-22 deal with events leading to the fall of Jerusalem. Verses 23-26 warn of false Christs which contributed to the Jewish War (A.D. 66-70). Verse 27 shows that Jesus' return will be seen by all. Verses 29-31 deal with the actual return of the Lord. Verses 32-36 actually involve both Jerusalem's fall and Jesus' return. The former he practically dates (v. 34). As this event is certain so will be his return. No man knows the time of his return (v. 36). Mark 13:32 adds "neither the Son, but the Father" (Acts 1:7). Verses 37-41 mean that life will pursue a normal course, until suddenly the Lord will come. At that time there will be a separation of the saved from the lost (Matt. 13:24-30,47-50). Verses 42-51 urge watchfulness for the Lord's return. The end of the age is the main thought in Matthew 25.

Some interpreters see several comings of Christ, two resurrections, and two or more judgments. The writer sees one of each. But one should not be dogmatic about one's position. The Bible tells all that is necessary, but not all that one may wish to know. See *Judgment; Millennium; Parousia.*

Eternal; Eternity. The finite mind of man is so bound to the *time* concept that he finds it difficult, if not impossible, to conceive of the ideas of the eternal and of eternity. But the Bible declares both. The Greek words used to express these concepts basically mean "age." This term carries a time concept, but the majority of Bible uses definitely extends beyond time as man reckons it. Yet in some contexts the idea of "world" or the present age is evident (Matt. 12:32; 13:22).

"Eternity" in the strictest sense is to be viewed apart from time—past, present, or future. It must be conceived of more in terms of God's being. He exists above time (2 Pet. 3:8), and yet he is concerned with time and man's needs. "For thus saith the high and lofty one that inhabiteth eternity, whose name is Holy; I dwell in the high and lofty place, with him also that is of a contrite and humble spirit" (Isa. 57:15). Thus Moses says, "The eternal God is thy refuge, and underneath are the everlasting arms" (Deut. 33:27).

The full revelation of such a God is seen in Jesus' concept of him as "Father." It is thus that he fills the void between eternity and time. God is above time and is unchangeable, yet he is involved in history as its God and with man as his Provider and Savior. To the believer he is Father in truth.

Even the peculiar name of Israel's God ["I AM" (Exod. 3:14b) and "I AM THAT I AM" (Exod. 3:14a)] involves the eternity-time concept. "I AM" expresses essential being, but it entails also the thought of God as the Eternal Present. With him there is no past or future. It is all *now*. Yet a literal translation of verse 14a, "He will be that which he will be," shows Jehovah's accommodation to man's time concept. He is revealing himself as Redeemer, which is his essential nature in his relation to man and which will be unfolded to man progressively until it reaches full meaning in Jesus Christ. And while man must never think of God as confined to time, neither must he regard him as unconcerned with time as man understands it. He is the eternal God. But he is also the refuge of time-bound man.

"Eternal" as used of the spiritual life of man should be seen in relation to both time and eternity. It is a quality of life which the believer receives now and which continues beyond time as men reckon it—or into eternity. Here, of course, for man this life is both present and future (John 3:15-16). Yet from God's viewpoint it is his imparting to man that quality of his divine nature which is in his essential being with no regard to time (John 1:12; Rom. 8:14-17).

Of interest is the fact that the Greek words for "eternal" are rendered in the New Testament as "eternal," "everlasting," and "for ever," or equivalents, at least one hundred and forty-five times. The phrase "unto the ages of the ages," the strongest Greek phrase for *eternal*, is used forty-two times—twenty-eight in Revelation.

As man stands in awe before the concept of eternity he can only say, "Now unto the King eternal, immortal, invisible, the only wise God, be honour, and glory for ever and ever [unto the ages of the ages]. Amen" (1 Tim. 1:17).

Evil; Evil Eye; Evil-Speaking. The Bible does not seek to explain the origin of evil. It recognizes its existence, and shows how God deals with it. In the Bible evil is presented as physical and moral.

Physical evil may come as God's punishment of sin: for example, the flood (Gen. 6:1 to 8:22) and the destruction of Sodom and Gomorrah (Gen. 18:20 to 19:25; see 2 Pet. 2:6). Isaiah lists certain places as marked for God's punishment: for instance, Babylon (13:1-22); Moab (15:1-9); Damascus (17:1-14); Egypt (19:1-17). See also Amos 1-2. In Isaiah 45:7 "create evil" does not mean that Jehovah is the source of evil. It means that he at times brings physical evil as punishment for sin.

This is not grounds for generalization as to all calamity and suffering. Job 1-2 clearly shows that Satan perpetrated evil upon Job, which God permitted in order that Job might be given the opportunity to clear his name of Satan's slander. Sometimes people, such as Job's children, suffer because of their relation to others. This explains the sufferings of Jesus and Paul. Each case must be judged upon its merits.

The emphasis in the New Testament is upon moral evil. James 1:13 clearly shows that God is not responsible for such. Moral evil is the fruit of man's rebellion against God and his inhumanity to man. Jesus notes that such evil is the overt expression of sinful hearts (Mark 7:21-23). He enlarges upon this in the Sermon on the Mount. In dealing with certain of the Commandments he showed their spiritual content as over against the overt act. The law against murder calls for a proper regard for human personality (Matt. 5:21-24). Adultery is first in the consent of the will whether or not one commits the act itself (Matt. 5:27-30). Love for one's neighbor includes his enemies as well as his friends (Matt. 5:43-47). The perfection in the character of God should be the gauge of character in the Christian (Matt. 5:48). Jesus condemned hypocrisy and called for positive virtue even in acts of charity and worship (Matt. 6:1-8,16-18; see Matt. 23). Words and deeds, whether good or bad, but show the condition of the heart (Matt. 12:33-37). Thus Jesus placed his emphasis upon the inner man with respect to both good and evil (Mark 7:20-23).

In the Bible the "evil eye" is synonymous with jealousy, envy, and covetousness (Matt. 20:15). In Matthew 6:22-23 (see Luke 11:34-36) Jesus compared the single eye with the evil eye. The single eye focuses upon true heavenly values. The evil eye is one with double vision, trying to focus on both heavenly and earthly values at the same time. One has called such cockeyed—one eye set on things of earth with the other rolled piously heavenward. Such fills the life with darkness; the single eye fills one with light. Light and darkness symbolize righteousness and evil respectively.

Evil-speaking is connoted by two words: one meaning speaking against or backbiting (Rom. 1:30; 2 Cor. 12:20; James 4:11), and the other meaning blasphemy or speaking insultingly against someone (Eph. 4:31; Col. 3:8; Jude 9). It involves slander. This latter word is involved in the unpardonable sin when related to slander of the Holy Spirit (Matt. 12:31-32). Since one is to be judged by his words, he should be careful how he speaks. See *Unpardonable Sin.*

Expedient. This translates a Greek word meaning to bear or bring together. It means to be profitable or well. In the New Testament it is never used in the sense of being opposed to what is right, with the possible exception of John 11:50; 18:14. The idea is that only that which is right is expedient. Thus it usually does not mean mere convenience as opposed to the right action. For examples of its use in this sense see Matthew 5:29-30; 19:10, "not good"; John 16:7; Acts 20:20, "be profitable"; 1 Corinthians 6:12; 7:35; 10:23,33; 12:7; 2 Corinthians 8:10; 12:1; Hebrews 12:10.

Fable; Myth. The Greek word so translated is Anglicized as "myth." It means a fable, myth, legend, story, or tale. It is found in the New Testament five times (1 Tim. 1:4; 4:7; 2 Tim. 4:4; Titus 1:14; 2 Pet. 1:16). Without exception it is used as the opposite of truth as found in the gospel. The exact meaning is not always clear. Paul refers to "Jewish fables" (Titus 1:14), perhaps false teachings concerning the person and work of Christ. 2 Peter 1:16 may be a reference to Gnostic philosophy which degraded Christ from deity to a created being. One group of Gnostics denied the deity of Jesus; another denied the humanity of Christ. Paul's other references may be to the same thing.

The term "myth" is used in certain schools of modern theology to refer to a literary vehicle for teaching truth: for instance, the myth of creation. Some theologians even seek to *demythologize* the Scriptures by removing accounts of the supernatural such as miracles and Jesus' virgin birth and resurrection. In the writer's opinion "myth" is an unfortunate term to use, for to the average person it means fable or fairy tale.

Faith; Faithful. The Greek words so translated are abundantly found in the New Testament: the verb, meaning to believe, trust, and commit, 248 times; the noun rendered "faith," 244 times; the adjective translated "faithful," 66 times. This is to be expected since the New Testament is a book of faith.

"Faith" means the ability of the heart to go farther than the eye can see or reason explore. It is one of the key words in Hebrews where it appears thirty-two times. Hebrew 11:1 reads, "Now faith is the substance [guarantee] of things hoped for, the evidence [convincing proof] of things not seen." This word also appears in Romans forty times (3:26, believe) and in Galatians twenty-two times. The emphasis of these letters is salvation by faith. Strangely this word does not appear in the Gospel of John and only seven times in the Johannine epistles and Revelation. But the verb form is found in John one hundred times. It is found ten times in 1 John, but does not appear in 2 and 3 John or Revelation. In James, the most practical book in the New Testament, "faith" appears sixteen times. Some see a conflict between Paul and James about saving faith (see James 2:14-26). However, it is simply a matter of emphasis and outlook. Paul insists that one is saved by faith. James says that saving faith will produce good works. Paul says the same thing in Ephesians 2:10 (see also Rom. 6:6-22).

The verb form for faith means to believe, to trust, and to commit (see John 2:24). In the sense of receiving Christ it means to believe the Gospel records about him to the point that in the will one trusts him for salvation and commits himself to his will and way of life. The inclusive word is *reliance*.

Faith then is reliance upon God in Christ with no claim to one's own merit (Rom. 4:1-3). It is joined with "grace" as the channel through which God's saving act in Christ flows into one's life. Grace is the Godward side; faith is the human response (Eph. 2:8-10). While man's work and merit are not the source, good works will be the result. But even this refers to the larger view of salvation of the Christian life. And it is a matter of God's grace and man's faith from beginning to end (John 1:16; Rom. 1:17). "The just shall live by faith" (Hab. 2:4) is the only Old Testament verse quoted three separate times in the New Testament (Rom. 1:17; Gal. 3:11; Heb. 10:38). "Faith" is also used of the body of truth which is the gospel (Acts 24:24; Gal. 1:23).

"Faithful" is an adjective which describes one facet of God's unchanging nature. And, of course, this nature is expressed in his work and relationships. God may change his method but never his ethical character or redemptive purpose. God is not slack concerning his promises (2 Pet. 3:9). This means that God honors his covenant relationship with his people (Rom. 3:3, "faith" here is the noun form). Though men may change, God does not change. This Paul applies to Christians in 2 Corinthians 1:18-22. Once one has exercised faith in Christ, he can know that God is faithful to keep his promise to save and keep safe. In 1 Corinthians 10:13. Paul assures his readers that it is through God's faithfulness that his people can resist temptation with assurance of his power to bear it.

Though God's promises may seem long in fulfilment (by man's calendar) one can have faith in God's faithfulness to perform (Heb. 11:11). Also 1 John 1:9 assures the confessing Christian that God is faithful to forgive and cleanse. The author of Hebrews ascribes this quality to Christ as our faithful high priest (2:17; 3:2). And as he is faithful, so should his people be faithful (Heb. 3:5).

In 1 Corinthians 1:9 Paul says that "God is faithful," trustworthy or worthy of trust. This together with 1 Corinthians 15:58 may be seen as parentheses enclosing Paul's discussions of the problems perplexing that church. He reminds his readers that God is worthy of their trust to lead them to the solution of the problems. "Therefore, my beloved brethren, be ye stedfast, unmoveable, always abounding in the work of the Lord, forasmuch as ye know that your labour is not in vain in the Lord." In effect, he says, "God is faithful . . . therefore, be ye faithful." See *Security of the Believer.*

Firstfruits. The offering of the firstfruits was a recognition that the land and its products were gifts from Jehovah. In the case of grain the first green heads of grain were plucked, dried by fire, and offered in thanksgiving for the anticipated general harvest about seven weeks later (Lev. 2:14-16; see Exod. 34:22-26). The Feast of Weeks or Pentecost celebrated the general harvest. This came fifty days after the Passover. The firstfruits thus were offered about Passover time.

This gives significance to Paul's words "But now is Christ risen from the dead, and become the firstfruits of them that slept" (1 Cor. 15:20). Jesus rose from the dead about the time of the offering of the firstfruits. So Paul pictures his resurrection as the firstfruits of which the general harvest will be the resurrection of the dead at his return (1 Cor. 15:23).

Flesh. This word was used at times to refer to bodies of animals and men. It is also found in the sense of mankind (Luke 3:6). The larger usage in the New Testament refers to flesh as opposed to spirit. The eternal Word who had existed as spirit "became flesh" (John 1:14; 1 Tim. 3:16). This distinction appears in all references to the incarnation of Christ (cf. 1 John 4:2). It is sometimes used of the natural life (Phil. 1:22,24). In Matthew 16:17 "flesh and blood" is used of current concepts of Christ as held by Jesus' contemporaries.

The New Testament does not regard actual flesh as essentially evil. Paul exhorted Christians to glorify God in their bodies (1 Cor. 6:20; "and in your spirit, which are God's" is not found in the best texts). The body of the Christian is the Holy of Holies of the Holy Spirit (1 Cor. 6:19).

Yet in 1 Corinthians Paul distinguishes between the natural, carnal, and spiritual man (2:14; 3:1,3). The natural man is the unregenerated man. The carnal Christian is one still under the control of his fleshly nature. (Flesh itself is not evil, but a nature that lives only to gratify the fleshly appetites is evil.) The spiritual man is a Christian controlled by the Holy Spirit. That flesh itself is not evil is shown in that Christ lived in a body of flesh (Heb. 2:14). Evil is not in flesh and blood as such, but in evil powers which try to work through men who become their tools (Eph. 6:12).

In 1 Corinthians 15:50-53 Paul shows that since the kingdom of God is spiritual, flesh and blood cannot inherit it. Those Christians who are alive at Christ's coming will be transformed into the bodies they will have in heaven (cf. 1 Cor. 15:35-49). The dead in Christ will be raised in their resurrection bodies (1 Thess. 4:13-17). See *Resurrection* and *Salvation*.

Fool. In the New Testament several words are rendered "fool" or "foolish." One means want of understanding (2 Tim. 3:9). Another means want of mind or wisdom (Mark 7:22; 2 Cor. 11:1). Another word is Anglicized as "moron," meaning dull or stupid (Matt. 7:26; 23:17; 25:2; 1 Cor. 1:25,27). Still another means no mind or sense (Luke 11:40; 12:20; Rom. 2:20, foolish; 1 Cor. 15:36; 2 Cor. 11:16,19; 12:6,11; Eph. 5:17, unwise; 1 Pet. 2:15, foolish). This is the word used to describe the rich fool (Luke 12:16-20). This man furnishes a good example of a "fool."

He was a fool because he failed to see God as the Lord of his harvest, and consulted no one else, not even God, as to what disposition to make of his goods. He was a fool because he thought only of himself. In three verses he used fourteen personal pronouns (KJV). He was a fool because he thought that he could feed his soul on things, and that he owned them when they owned him. He thought he would live so long, when life was so short. The Greek text reads, "Fool, this night your soul [or life] they [things] are requiring from you" (v. 20). Whether he died that night or lived for many years, his soul was being required of him by things. Money is a great servant, but it is a terrible master.

Foot Washing. See *Washing of Feet.*

Foreknowledge. This is the term used by theologians to refer to the fact that in his *omniscience* (which see) God knows beforehand the entire course of events which from the human viewpoint lie in the future. The Greek verb is used five times in the New Testament where it is variously rendered as "foreknow" (Rom. 8:29; 11:2); "know" (Acts 26:5); "foreordain" (1 Pet. 1:20); and "know before" (2 Pet. 3:17). The noun form is used twice as "foreknowledge" (Acts 2:23; 1 Pet. 1:2).

However, foreknowledge of an event does not necessarily mean that one causes it. One must ever reckon with the fact of man's free will. For instance, God knows beforehand who will receive or reject Christ. But he wills that all should come to repentance and life (2 Pet. 3:9). Yet man is free to choose, being held responsible for his choices.

God's foreknowledge must be viewed in the light of his eternal purpose of redemption (Eph. 3:10-11). God is the God of history (Acts 17:26-31). He is not responsible for the evil of men and nations. But he guides the course of human history toward the accomplishment of his benevolent, redemption purpose. It is precisely his foreknowledge which enables him to guide events, overruling the evil and working all things for good to those who love him and who fit into his benevolent purpose (Rom. 8:28).

Man sees history in segments. The all-wise God sees it all with one sweeping glance. What man calls the future—God is already there. It is for this reason that Christians can face with confidence the humanly unknown. In the old adage, he does not know what the future holds; but he knows who holds the future. Thus God's foreknowledge is a source of comfort to those who trust him. It is in this light that Jesus can say, "In this world ye shall have tribulation: but be of good cheer [courage]; I have overcome [fully conquered] the world" (John 16:33). See *Election.*

Foreordination. The Greek verb from which the noun comes means to set a boundary beforehand. From the basic verb comes the word "horizon." The verb appears in the New Testament six times: Romans 8:29-30; Ephesians 1:5,11 where it is rendered "predestinate"; Acts 4:28 as "determine before"; and 1 Corinthians

2:7 as "ordain."

This doctrine does not mean fatalism. It does not ignore the free will of man (Acts 2:23). The idea of the saving of souls being predestinated (Rom. 8:29-30; Eph. 1:5,11) means that God has beforehand, or before the foundation of the world, set a boundary "in Christ" for all who will be saved. Every person is free to choose whether he will be "in Christ" or outside Christ (see *Election*).

In the course of events in history God has set a boundary beforehand by which, while *permitting* events contrary to his will, he guides history toward the accomplishment of his benevolent purpose. For instance, Judas was responsible for his betrayal of Jesus (Luke 22:22), but God used it to redemptive ends. The same may be said of all involved in the Lord's death. But in his death and resurrection God overruled their evil to provide redemption for a lost world.

It may be difficult for some to separate the idea of foreordination from the inevitability of every single event. But along with God's sovereignty one must place the equally biblical truth of man's free will. As a person man is not a puppet on a string. He acts with conscious knowledge and attendant responsibility. But God guides and overrules to the accomplishment of his purpose. A righteous God will always do right.

Forgiveness. There are four Greek words used to denote forgiveness. One means "to loose from" (Luke 13:12). Another is rendered "remission" (Rom. 3:25, only use in N. T.). One of the principal words means "putting away." It is used seventeen times in the New Testament in various renderings: "remission" (Matt. 26:28; Mark 1:4; Luke 1:77; 3:3; 24:47; Acts 2:38; 10:43; Heb. 9:22; 10:18); "forgiveness" (Mark 3:29; Acts 5:31; 13:38; 26:18; Eph. 1:7; Col. 1:14); "deliverance" and "liberty" (Luke 4:18). This word carries the idea of complete forgiveness. The fourth word is the verb form of "grace." It means to grace someone. Used only by Luke (seven times) and Paul (sixteen times) it emphasizes God's grace in forgiveness. (See Luke 7:42-43; Rom. 8:32; Col. 2:13). Paul also uses it of Christians forgiving each other (2 Cor. 2:7,10; 12:13; Eph. 4:32; Col. 3:13, note double use in this last reference).

Of course, God's forgiveness is neither arbitrary nor universal.

It is based upon the grounds of forgiveness created in the atonement wrought through his Son. And it is granted only to those who in repentance and faith receive his Son as Savior. Forgiveness is in God's heart, or else there would have been no atonement. However, a holy, righteous God cannot ignore sin. Having paid the price for sin, he graciously bestows it upon all who will receive it through repentance and faith.

The same may be said of forgiveness on the part of a Christian. The offended party should have a forgiving attitude. But for it to be personally effected in the offender he must repent and ask forgiveness. Furthermore, the offended one should seek the offender's repentance (Matt. 18:15-17). It is only when every effort proves fruitless that the offended one may accept it as a hopeless case. As often as one offends and repents, he is to be forgiven (Luke 17:3-4).

In Matthew 18:21 Peter asked how often he should forgive one—"till seven times?" The rabbis required only three times. So Peter thought he was being generous. Jesus' reply "Until seventy times seven" (v. 22) should not be taken mathematically. The point is unlimited forgiveness.

In Matthew 18:23-35 Jesus strongly condemns an unforgiving spirit in those who have received such great forgiveness from God. And in the incident of the sinful woman in Luke 7:37-47 he shows that one's love for him should be in proportion to the forgiveness received from him.

Ephesians 4:32 puts human and divine forgiveness in the proper proportion. Literally, "Gracing one another even as also God in Christ graced you." See *Atonement; Grace; Salvation.*

Fulness. The Greek word so translated comes from a verb which means to fill. The noun *plērōma* means variously the thing filled, that which fills, and ultimately a fulfilling or "fulness." This word is used seventeen times in the New Testament. Thirteen times it is translated "fulness" (John 1:16; Rom. 11:12,25; 15:29; 1 Cor. 10:26,28; Gal. 4:4; Eph. 1:10,23; 3:19; 4:13; Col. 1:19; 2:9). Paul alone uses it in this sense twelve times. In Romans it speaks of God's purpose in dealing with Gentiles and Jews. In Galatians 4:4 the "fulness of the time" means a time that was right in God's eyes (Eph. 1:10).

Elsewhere in Ephesians and Colossians it may be seen as the very essence of Christ or God. For instance, the church as Christ's body is all of him that men see with the natural eye between his ascension and return (Eph. 1:23). The goal of the church and the Christian is to be filled with the essence of Christ and/or God (Eph. 3:19; 4:13).

Paul's use in Colossians is of the greatest significance (see John 1:16). Both Paul and John were writing to refute Gnostic philosophy. This philosophy regarded God as absolutely good and matter as absolutely evil. Its problem was how to explain the origin of the universe. How could an absolutely good God create absolutely evil matter? To them the solution lay in positing a series of created beings in descending order out of God, each having less deity than the one above it. The lowest being had enough deity to create, but so little as to be able to create evil matter. A favorite term of the Gnostics was "fulness." It was this state that one achieved as he advanced upward in their system of knowledge.

When they came into contact with Christianity, they identified Christ as the lowest of these beings. This regarded him as a demigod, almost a demon. Obviously this cut straight across the Christian concept of the person and work of Christ. John declared him to be the eternal Word, equal with God, even God himself, who created the universe in every part (1:1-3). Furthermore, he became flesh for man's salvation (John 1:14). In him resided the very essence of deity (fulness) which he imparts to all who believe in him (John 1:12,16).

In Colossians Paul says essentially the same thing (1:15-17,19). In this creator-Christ, the head of the church, is at home the very essence of deity. So both John and Paul took this pet term of the Gnostics and used it against them.

Perhaps the greatest statement as to the deity of Jesus Christ is found in Colossians 2:9. Literally, "Because in him alone is permanently at home every single part of the essence of deity [the fulness], the state of being God, in bodily form." Anyone who denies the deity of Jesus or the humanity of Christ speaks with the Gnostics. They also contradict the clear teachings of both John and Paul. See *Gnosticism.*

Gehenna. Gehenna is a transliteration from the Aramaic (language spoken by Palestinian Jews in Jesus' day) form of the Hebrew meaning "valley of Hinnom." The prevailing name in the Old Testament is "the valley of the son of Hinnom" (Jer. 19:2). In the King James Version this name is translated as "hell." See *Hades.*

It is a valley south of the city of Jerusalem. Once it had been the site of the worship of the Canaanite fire god Molech (2 Chron. 28:3; 33:6). In its worship infants were burned to death by placing them in a fire in his arms. In his religious reforms Josiah destroyed the idol and defiled the valley. By the time of Jesus this valley was used as the garbage dump of Jerusalem. In this valley was thrown all the waste of the city, including the bodies of dead animals and of executed criminals which were unclaimed.

To consume the garbage fires burned constantly. Maggots worked in the filth. At night wild dogs came to eat the edible portions of garbage. As they fought over it they howled and gnashed their teeth. At times the wind blew the stench of this place into the city. It was a place of utter defilement. Jeremiah used it as a figure of judgment upon Judah (7:32).

Jesus adopted Gehenna as a figure of hell as a place of punishment. The word *Gehenna* is found twelve times in the New Testament. Other than James 3:6 it appears only in the Gospels, and always from the lips of Jesus (Matt. 5:22,29-30; 10:28; 18:9; 23:15,33; Mark 9:43,45,47; Luke 12:5). At times even when he did not use the word itself, it is clear that he had it in mind (Matt. 13:42,50; Mark 9:43-45,46,48). In a sense Jesus says that hell is God's cosmic garbage dump. What is unfit for heaven is cast into hell (Rev. 21:8; 22:15).

The fact that only he who is the essence of love and mercy used this word as a place of punishment adds all the more to its horror. God sends no man to hell. In Christ he has done all that even he can do to prevent it. If one goes to hell he does it of his own free will. See *Hell.*

Gifts of the Holy Spirit. These gifts were bestowed upon Christians in the early church to be used in specific services for the Lord. In 1 Corinthians 12:8-10,28-29 one finds the most exhaustive list. But Paul mentions other lists in Romans 12:6-8; Ephesians 4:11. In 1 Corinthians 12—14 he discusses problems growing out of the abuse of these spiritual gifts. He says that the Spirit has distributed them "to every man severally as he will." The proper use of these gifts he likens to a well-organized and effective body (1 Cor. 12:14-30). These gifts are to be exercised in Christian love (1 Cor. 13). See *Love* and *Tongues, Speaking in.*

Glory. In the New Testament this word renders the Greek word *doxa* whence comes the English word "doxology." It carries the idea of brightness, brilliance, and splendor. In a literal sense it is used of the heavenly bodies (1 Cor. 15:41). When used of men it denotes rank and power, such as "Solomon in all his glory" (Matt. 6:20; see Matt. 4:8; Rev. 21:24,26). It also connotes the praise or honor given by men to men (John 5:41,44). Paul uses it in the sense of distinction to himself with regard to the fruit of his labors (1 Thess. 2:20). Even his sufferings he describes as his glory (Eph. 3:13).

The concept of brilliance, power, and splendor is also evident in "glory" ascribed to God. The angels sang of God's glory at the birth of Jesus (Luke 2:14). God's glory is revealed in his creative work, even though evil men did not glorify him for it (Rom. 1:21; cf. Psalm 19:1). But God's greatest glory is seen in his redemptive work in Christ (Phil. 2:11; see John 12:28). Thus glory is repeatedly ascribed to him in the epistles (Rom. 11:36; 16:27; Gal. 1:5; Eph. 1:6,12,14; 2 Tim. 4:18; Heb. 13:21; 1 Pet. 5:11). This glory is ascribed to both God and Christ (Rev. 4-5; see also John 1:14). Jesus prayed that God would give to him the glory which was his before his incarnation (John 17:5). God exalted him above and beyond that upon his return to heaven as the Redeemer (Phil. 2:9). Jesus spoke of his death and resurrection in terms of being glorified (John 12:23).

The words "glorify" and "glory" are also used of "saints" or Christians (Luke 9:31; see 2 Cor. 3:7-11,18 where Paul contrasts God's glory reflected temporarily in Moses' face with the abiding and increasing glory in Christ and his people). "Glory" is used with respect to heaven where the Lord's people share his glory (Matt. 16:27; Luke 24:26; Rom. 8:17-18,21; 2 Cor. 4:17-18).

The Greek word for "glory" appears one hundred and sixty-eight times in the New Testament, the vast majority of which refer to the glory of God, Christ, and his people. This shows the great emphasis which the New Testament places upon the brilliance, splendor, and praiseworthiness of the Lord. What a privilege to share in this glory!

Gnosticism. Gnosticism as such is not mentioned in the New Testament. One possible allusion to it is found in 1 Timothy 6:20-21 where Paul warns against "profane and vain babblings, and oppositions of science [*gnōsis*, knowledge] so called: which some professing have erred concerning the faith." Timothy was in Ephesus in the general area where an incipient Gnosticism flourished at the time. Such teaching is reflected in various New Testament writings.

Gnosticism was a syncretism of various religions and philosophies: for instance, Platonic philosophy, religions of Persia and India, plus elements of Judaism. It regarded God as absolutely good and matter as absolutely evil. Its problem was to explain the origin of matter or the universe and also the salvation of the soul. But as one has said, it was more concerned with saving philosophers from matter than men from sin.

How could an absolutely good God create absolutely evil matter? To answer this question these philosophers posited a series of beings emanating from God in descending order, with each being having less deity than the one above it. The lowest of these beings, which they called the Demiurge, possessed enough deity to create but so little as to be able to create evil matter.

When they came into contact with Christianity, they identified Christ as the Demiurge. Thus they considered him a created being, a demigod or almost a demon. The Gnostics were divided into two groups concerning the person of Jesus Christ. The Docetics (from a Greek word for "seem") held that Christ did not have a real flesh and blood body, but only *seemed* to have. The Cerinthian Gnostics, named for their leader Cerinthus, held that Christ was not born nor did he die. His deity came upon Jesus at his baptism and left him on the cross. The one denied the humanity of Christ;

the other denied the deity of Jesus. Naturally this cut across Christian Christology.

To the Gnostics salvation was obtained by achieving various ascending levels of knowledge or *gnōsis*. The completed state they called "fulness" or *plērōma*, a favorite word of theirs. Their attitude toward the absolute separation of spirit as good and matter as evil produced two results: asceticism or complete separation from matter for some; licentiousness for others since to them what the body did did not affect the spirit. These things present the barest outline of a very complicated system (see *The International Standard Bible Encyclopaedia,* Vol. II., pp. 1240-1248).

That this philosophy posed a great threat to Christian truth is seen in the fact that so much of the New Testament deals with refuting it. Both Colossians and the Gospel of John insist upon the essential deity-humanity of Jesus Christ (John 1:1,14; 10:30; Col. 1:15-17; 2:9), his work in creation (John 1:3; Col. 1:16), his *fulness* which he gives to his people (John 1:14b,16; Col. 1:19; 2:9-10), and his death for man's sin (John 19:18-34; Col. 1:20). The examples are so many as to require a complete reading of these books. The same is true of 1 John, which speaks against those who deny that Jesus Christ came in flesh as God's Son (1 John 1:1-3; 4:1-3), those who claim sinlessness or else live licentiously (1 John 1:5-10; 2:15-17), and that while the Gnostics went out from the Christian group they are none of it (1 John 2:19). John's emphasis on love for each other reflects the cold intellectualism of the Gnostics with no love for men (1 John 4:7-12).

This is also true of the Pastoral Epistles. Various aspects of Gnostic teachings and practices are reflected in such passages as 1 Timothy 2:4-6; 4:3-4; 2 Timothy 3:19b-23; 3:1-7,9,13; and Titus 1:16. See also 2 Peter 2:1-3,10,12-21. Jude is directed against the licentiousness of Gnosticism (see verses 3-4,8,10-13,16,19). Evidence of certain Gnostic practices are also found in Revelation. The Nicolaitans and Balaamites (Rev. 2:14-15) probably were elements of Gnosticism. "The depths" (Rev. 2:24) was a phrase used by Gnostics who claimed to be superior to ordinary believers. "The depths of Satan" probably means the licentious teaching that sins of the body do not affect the spirit.

Unfortunately Gnosticism is not dead. All who deny the deity of Jesus (e.g. his virgin birth and bodily resurrection) or the humanity of Christ (e.g. the atoning death) are Gnostics. The same may be said of those who worship their intellects rather than God, who practice asceticism as a means of salvation, or live licentiously. These do not represent advanced thought but ancient Gnostic philosophy. See *Fulness.*

God. The Bible does not seek to prove the existence of God. It assumes that he is (Gen. 1:1). Belief in God or gods is seen throughout its pages. Only two verses deal with the so-called atheist (Psalms 14:1; 53:1). Note that a "fool" or unthinking person says in his *heart,* "There is no God." In his *mind* he knows better. In his *will* he wishes there were no God to whom he is responsible. The Bible says that all mankind once had a knowledge of the true God, but in rebellion many rejected him for paganism with all its evils (Gen. 1-4; Rom. 1-2).

E. Y. Mullins (*The Christian Religion in Its Doctrinal Expression,* pp. 214-15) defines God as "the supreme personal Spirit; perfect in all his attributes; who is the source, support, and end of the universe; who guides it according to the wise, righteous, and loving purpose revealed in Jesus Christ; who indwells in all things by his Holy Spirit, seeking ever to transform them according to his own will and bring them to the goal of his kingdom."

The general name for God or gods in the Old Testament is *Elohim.* (Gen. 1:1; 1 Kings 18:21,24), probably meaning "a putter forth of power." It is a plural form of majesty, and possibly carries the idea of the Trinity. This word appears 2,550 times. The short form *El* is used in combination with other words to denote certain aspects of his nature: God Almighty (Gen. 17:1); the most high God (Gen. 14:19); the everlasting God (Gen. 21:33). The Greek equivalent of *Elohim* is *Theos. Adonai* (340 times in the O.T.) is rendered "Lord." Of God it means a helper in time of need (Gen. 15:2,8). "Jehovah" is the peculiar name of Israel's God, and appears in the Old Testament 6,823 times. In the King James Version it is rendered as "Lord" (Psalm 23:1). Often it is used in connection with *Elohim* to show that the God who did a thing was the true God (Gen. 2:3-4,7). In the New Testament *Kurios,* Lord, refers to Jehovah or when used of Jesus in the purely Christian sense as Jehovah in flesh. Jehovah is God's redeeming name. It is formed out of the Hebrew verb "to be" (Exod. 3:14; note the "I ams" of Jesus).

Jehovah is one (Deut. 6:4), but manifests himself as Father, Son, and Holy Spirit. Jesus said, "God is a Spirit" (John 4:24). But he has revealed himself in flesh as Jesus Christ (John 1:14; 10:30; 14:9).

God's attributes are described as *natural* (seven) and *moral* (four). He is *self-existent* or exists by reason of what he is within himself (Gen. 1:1); *immutable* or does not change in character, nature, and purpose (Mal. 3:6; Heb. 13:8); *omnipresent* or is present simultaneously in all space and time (Psalm 139:7-12); *immense* or is not confined to or limited by space (Isa. 57:15); *eternal* or has no beginning or end (Rev. 1:8); *omniscient* or all-wise (Rom. 11:33-36); *omnipotent* or is all-powerful to act in keeping with his nature, character, and purpose (Gen. 17:1; 18:14). His moral attributes are *holiness* (Lev. 11:44; Isa. 6:1-3), *righteousness* (Rom. 1:17; 3:26), *truth* (Rom. 11:33-36), and *love* (1 John 4:7-10). These relate to all his other attributes, and love qualifies all his nature and deeds.

Jesus revealed God as "Father" (Matt. 11:25-26; John 1:18). He is fatherly in his nature, longs to be Father to all men, but is such in truth only to those who have believed in his Son. See *Jesus Christ; Holy Spirit.*

Godhead. This word occurs three times in the New Testament, and translates three different but kindred Greek words (Acts 17:29; Rom. 1:20; Col. 2:9). These words connote all that is involved in deity. In Acts 17:29 the word is rendered "Deity" in the Revised Standard Version, probably in contrast to pagan deities which abounded in Athens. In Romans 1:20 RSV the word is rendered "deity" but preceded by "God." Here Paul says that the reality of God is evidenced in the natural order. The apostle's strongest use of "Godhead" is found in Colossians 2:9. It may read "every single part of deity [the state of being God]" permanently dwells in Christ alone in bodily form. This statement is directed against the Gnostics whose system practically emptied Jesus of deity and denied the full incarnation of Christ. Colossians 2:9 is possibly the strongest declaration of the deity of Jesus Christ found in the New Testament.

Golgotha. This word is from the Aramaic, and is translated into Greek as "the place of a skull" (Matt. 27:33; Mark 15:22; John 19:17). Luke 23:33 calls it "Calvary" though the Greek word for *skull* is used. One explanation of the name is that it was a place for public execution and had skulls lying about. Due to Jewish insistence upon burial this is unlikely. Probably the contour of the ground resembled a skull.

Many places have been suggested as the site of Jesus' crucifixion. But today the prominent ones are the site of the Church of the Holy Sepulcher and Gordon's Calvary, which is atop the Grotto of Jeremiah. Arguments are advanced for both sites. Gordon's Calvary looks like a skull. The records simply say that it was outside the city walls (Heb. 13:12), near a public road (Matt. 27:39; John 19:20) leading from the country into the city (Mark 15:40; Luke 23:49). Archaeology has not definitely determined the location of the city wall at that time. No one can be certain as to the place. Perhaps God does not intend that it should be known. Christianity is not to be tethered to a place, but is to cover the earth. The location of Jesus' tomb is linked to that of Golgotha.

Goodness. This word translates three Greek words in the New Testament. Two have the idea respectively of "usefulness" and "benignity" (Rom. 2:4; 11:22); or "useful," "benign," "kind" (Luke 6:35; Rom. 2:4). The third word means "full of good" (Rom. 15:14; Gal. 5:22; Eph. 5:9; 2 Thess. 1:11).

Gospel. This word is derived from the Anglo-Saxon word "Godspel" meaning "good news concerning God." The Greek word means "good news." In the general sense it refers to the totality of the message concerning God's redemptive work in Jesus Christ (Mark 1:1; Acts 20:24). Mark's usage in 1:1 relates it to the events in the life of Jesus Christ. The Greek word has been Anglicized into "evangel," "evangelist," and "evangelism."

In the New Testament the word is never strictly used for a book, but refers to various aspects of God's redeeming word in Christ: e.g. "the gospel of God" (Rom. 1:1); "the gospel" (Rom. 1:16, "of Christ" not in best texts); "the gospel of Christ" (Rom. 15:19; 1 Cor. 9:12); "the gospel of the grace of God" (Acts 20:24); "the gospel of peace" (Eph. 6:15); "the gospel of your salvation" (Eph. 1:13); "the glorious gospel of Christ" (2 Cor. 4:4).

There is, therefore, a distinction between "law" and "gospel." Strictly speaking "law" is what God tells man to do. "Gospel" tells what God has graciously done for man (Acts 15:11).

In time the capitalized form "Gospel" came to be used for the four accounts of the life and ministry of Jesus Christ. Matthew, Mark, and Luke are called the "Synoptic Gospels," since they relate their accounts from the same point of view. "Synoptic" means "seeing together." Mark was the first to be written. The other two follow its general framework, but add portions of their own. John is called the Fourth Gospel to distinguish it from the other three. See *Preach.*

Grace. This is one of the most wonderful words in the New Testament. Its meaning for men is even more wonderful. The noun form is used one hundred and fifty-six times. The verb is found twenty-three times, eleven of them translated "forgive." The English word "charisma" is a transliteration of the Greek word rendered seventeen times as "gift" (cf. Rom. 1:11; 6:23) or "free gift" (Rom. 5:15-16). The noun *charis* is translated one hundred and thirty times as "grace" (cf. John 1:14; Eph. 2:7-8). In Luke 4:22 "gracious" may well read "charm" of Jesus' words (see Col. 4:6). "Favour" (Luke 1:30; 2:52) translates this word. "Thank" in Luke 17:9 reads, literally, "have grace." In 1 Corinthians 16:3 this word refers to money given as a "liberality."

With reference to salvation "grace" basically means a gift. In this sense the derivation of the meaning is to make a gift, to forgive a debt, to forgive a wrong, to forgive sin. So God's salvation in Christ is basically his gift apart from man's work or merit (Eph. 2:8-10). Good works are the *fruit* and not the *root* of salvation. Salvation cannot be by grace and works. The two cancel out each other. As one has said, grace means that God has done for you what neither you, nor anyone, nor anything else could do for you. So grace negates anything done by or to one by another person for his salvation.

"Grace" is also used with respect to God's gifts, which enable one to serve him (1 Cor. 1:4; Eph. 4:7). Paul uses it to refer to his gift from God to be the apostle to the Gentiles (Eph. 3:2,7-8). The *gifts* given to the Corinthians are called *charismas* (1 Cor. 12:4-10). In 1 Corinthians 4:7 Paul asks, "What hast thou that thou didst not receive?" as a gift from God. One's gifts should be a means for service, not the basis of inordinate pride. This is true whether it be salvation or the ability to serve the Lord.

"Grace" is also used of God's sustaining power in trouble (2 Cor. 12:9; 2 Tim. 2:1). So *grace* reminds us that all we have and are should be grounds of thanksgiving to God (1 Cor. 15:10). See *Atonement; Faith;* and *Salvation.*

Grace, Falling from. This is a belief held by some to the effect that one can be saved and then lost again, so that he must be saved again. While many verses of Scripture are said to teach this, the term comes from Galatians 5:4. "Christ is become of no effect unto you, whosoever of you are justified by the law [Greek, in law]; ye are fallen from grace."

This verse must be examined in the context of the entire epistle. Paul is arguing against the Judaizers (Acts 15:1) who insisted that Gentiles must first become Jews in religion, then believe in Jesus for salvation. He preached salvation by grace through faith (Eph. 2:8-10), whereas they taught a salvation by law or works plus faith. So since Paul held to salvation by grace, the last thing he would intend to say is that one can be saved and then lose it because of evil works.

"Become of no effect" really means "become inoperative." Christ is not in the business of saving by legalism but by grace. "Are justified" should read "are trying to be justified." "Law" has no definite article, so it can mean any law: Mosaic or other code. The Greek text reads "in the sphere of law" or legalism. The verb rendered "fallen from" really reads "fallen out of." "Ye did fall out of grace." The picture is not one in grace falling from it. Rather it regards one's choice whether to be saved by legalism or by grace. If one chooses the road of legalism, he rejects the road of grace. It is a matter of such never having been in grace.

Certain passages in Hebrews are cited as teaching falling from grace (2:1ff.; 3:7ff.; 6:1ff.; 10:19ff.; 12:1ff.). But in the context of the epistle they allow a different meaning—failure to develop and fulfil one's place in God's world mission of redemption (Herschel H. Hobbs, *How to Follow Jesus* [Nashville: Broadman, 1971]). It should be noted that if one holds Hebrews 6:1ff. as teaching falling from grace, then it also teaches that one can never be saved again.

Over against such verses one should note: John 3:16; 5:24; 10:28-29; Ephesians 1:13-14; 2:8-10; Colossians 3:3. The overall teaching of the New Testament abundantly teaches the security of the believer. See *Security of the Believer*.

Hades. *Hades* is Greek for the abode or state of the dead, corresponding to "Sheol" in the Old Testament. Unfortunately, with one exception (1 Cor. 15:55), the King James Version renders it as "hell." Except where the word "hell" translates *Gehenna* (which see), it means simply that one dies and enters into the realm of death. For instance, Acts 2:27 means that Christ's body will not be left to decay in death or the tomb. Capernaum will simply die as a city (Matt. 11:23). The "gates of Hades" or death will not contain Christ's church (Matt. 16:18).

In Luke 16:22-23 both Lazarus and the rich man died or entered Hades. But there is a difference. Beyond death Lazarus is the honored guest at the heavenly banquet; the rich man is in torment or in Gehenna. Here "hell" renders "Hades."

Hades is never used in the sense of a final state of the wicked. The idea of hell as a place of punishment is expressed in *Gehenna* and "the lake of fire" (Rev. 20:15). See *Hell*.

Har-Magedon; Armageddon. "Har-Magedon" is the Greek form of the Hebrew *Har-Meghiddō*, "Mount of Megiddo." It is found in the New Testament as "Armageddon" (Rev. 16:16).

This mountain overlooks the plain of Esdraelon. Because of its large level area this plain was the site of numerous battles (Judges 5:19; 2 Kings 23:29; 2 Chron. 35:22). Perhaps more blood has been shed here than on any other comparable area.

In Revelation 16:13-16 three unclean frogs out of the mouth of the dragon (Satan), the beast (Rome), and the false prophet (the group enforcing emperor worship) gather together at Armageddon the armies of those opposing Christ for the final battle of the age. This battle is described in Revelation 19:11-21. Note that Christ and his army ride upon white horses, symbolic of victory. His army, the saints, are clothed not in armor but in white linen, symbolic of victory and vindication. None is armed. Christ's only arm is the sword proceeding from his mouth. It is the sword of the Spirit, the word of God (Eph. 6:17). The beast and false prophet are cast into the lake of fire. The army opposing Christ is slain by the sword out of his mouth. Complete victory over his enemies!

These passages in Revelation are apocalyptic or symbolic language (Rev. 1:1, "signified" or sign-i-fied). Many see this as a literal battle. But the symbolism suggests that Christ's victory is won, not with material weapons, but with the spiritual weapon—the sword of the Spirit which is the word of God or the gospel. In any event the truth taught is the final and complete victory of Christ over all who oppose him. Note Revelation 20:7-10.

Hate. In its basic sense hate is a strong and evil attitude toward others. Such an attitude is condemned in both the Old and New Testaments (Num. 35:20-21; Prov. 10:12; 1 John 3:15). Jesus warned against a wrong attitude toward another (Matt. 5:21-22) as the source of murder. He taught that one should rather love all men, even his enemies (Matt. 5:43-47). One does not have to agree with another to love him in the Christian sense (Rom. 5:8).

The word "hate" is also used to express choice or a strong preference of one person over another. In this sense God loved Jacob, but hated Esau (Mal. 1:3; Rom. 9:13). Likewise, one should *hate* father and mother in comparison to Christ—not a malevolent attitude but a choice. See *Love*.

Heaven. While later Judaism spoke of seven heavens, the general idea was three heavens: where birds fly; where clouds are; where God dwells. It is in this last sense that heaven interests the Christian. It is the eternal abode of the redeemed (John 14:2-3). The Jews thought of heaven as a banquet with Abraham as the host (Luke 17:22). When Jesus spoke of "Paradise" he evidently referred to heaven (Luke 23:43; see Rev. 22). Paul was caught up into "the third heaven" which apparently also refers to Paradise (2 Cor. 12:2).

Revelation 21:1 speaks of "a new heaven and a new earth, for the first heaven and the first earth were passed away." Verse 2 sees the new Jerusalem coming down from God out of heaven. 2 Peter 3:12-13 speaks of the heavens being dissolved with fervent heat and of "a new heaven and a new earth, wherein dwelleth righteousness." Apparently these figures refer to a redeemed cosmic order (Rom. 8:22; 1 Cor. 15:25-28). Certainly one should not see heaven as God's dwelling place passing away. All of this is eschatological language, and one finds difficulty in pressing details. The Bible does not tell all one wishes to know, but all he needs to know.

But one thing is certain. God's *heaven* is the home of the redeemed (2 Cor. 5:1). It is not simply a state but a place. Where is heaven? It is where Jesus is. And that is heaven enough! See *Kingdom of God; of Heaven;* and *Paradise.*

Heir. An heir is one who receives an inheritance from another (Mark 12:7). In the Christian sense it means the inheritance Christians receive from God. In the New Testament the verb form is found eighteen times, all but two being rendered "inherit" (Matt. 5:5). One noun from this verb is used fourteen times, always as "inheritance" (Eph. 1:14,18; 5:5). The noun "heir" is found fifteen times (Rom. 8:17). This word is used in the compound form four times: "fellow-heir" (Eph. 3:6); "joint-heir" (Rom. 8:17); "heir together" (1 Pet. 3:7); "heir with" (Heb. 11:9). A true reading of Ephesians 1:11 means that Christians are God's inheritance (but see 1:14).

For the Christian the richest use of this idea is in Romans 8:17. In this passage Paul draws upon the Roman law of adoption. An adopted son became a joint-heir with natural sons. So as such believers are God's children, "then heirs; heirs of God, and joint-heirs with Christ; if so be that we suffer with him, that we may be also glorified together." Note that we are heirs of both his suffering and glory. But the suffering is not to be compared with the glory (v. 18). See *New Birth; Adoption.*

Hell. "Hell" in the King James Version renders both *hades* and *Gehenna* (which see). Gehenna refers to hell as a place of everlasting punishment for the lost. "Hell fire" (Matt. 5:22) renders "Gehenna of fire." This suggests the "lake of fire" (Rev. 20:10,15). The question is often asked as to whether or not hell is a literal fire. The Bible so describes it (Luke 16:24). It uses the most excruciating suffering to describe hell. If fire be regarded as symbolic, one should get no comfort from this. The reality is always greater than the symbol, whether it describes the glory of heaven (Rev. 21-22) or the horror of hell.

One time in the New Testament "to cast down to hell" translates the verb "to cast down [send] to Tartarus" (2 Pet. 2:4; note Matt. 25:41; Jude 6). Peter describes this as a place of punishment for fallen angels. But this probably also means hell as a place of punishment. See *Punishment, Everlasting*.

Herods. Since this family figures so greatly in the New Testament, a brief word should be said about them. Herod the Great, an Idumaean, ruled in Palestine B.C. 37-4 under the Romans (Matt. 2:3). He had ten wives, but the children of only four figure in New Testament history. Herod Antipas was tetrarch (ruler of a fourth of a kingdom) of Galilee and Perea (Luke 3:1). One son, Herod Philip, was a private citizen (Mark 6:17). Another by the same name was tetrarch of Iturea and Trachonitis (Luke 3:1), after whom Caesarea Philippi was named. Archelaus ruled over Judea 4 B.C.-A.D. 6 when he was deposed by the Romans (Matt. 2:22). Herod Agrippa I (Acts 12:1,6,19-23) and Herodias (Mark 6:17) were children of Aristobulus, one of Herod the Great's sons. Agrippa ruled as king of Judea A.D. 40-44. He was the father of Herod Agrippa II, king of Calchis, and Bernice (Acts 25:13,23). They lived together as man and wife. Also Drusilla was a daughter of Agrippa I and the wife of Felix the Roman procurator (Acts 24:24).

Herodians. They were a political party whose aim was to restore a Herod to the throne of Judaea and other areas formerly ruled by Herod the Great (Matt. 22:16; Mark 3:6). Though they were political foes of the Pharisees who wished to restore the Davidic kingdom, they joined them in their common cause against Jesus. "The leaven of Herod" (Mark 8:15) could refer to Herod Antipas or to the Herodians. See *Christian*.

Hireling. In both Testaments this word refers to one who works for a wage (Job 7:1; Isa. 16:14; 21:16). The Greek word in the New Testament is used only four times: "hired servant" (Mark 1:20; John 10:12-13). In John Jesus the good Shepherd compares himself to the hired servants. Their concern is for wages, not sheep. The shepherd gives his life protecting his sheep. A kindred word is rendered "hired servant" in Luke 15:17,19. The prodigal son did not expect to be restored to sonship. He did not want to be even a slave but a hired servant. A slave had economic security. A hired servant could be dismissed at any time.

Holiness; Holy. "Holiness" is related to "holy." The biblical idea in the words is that of separation from the world and worldly use.

Originally in extrabiblical use "holy" applied to any person or thing set apart for the service of a god. Women used in the worship of sex deities were called "holy" women. It was when the word came to be used of God that it took on his moral and ethical qualities. But even in the Bible the idea of the separation of things and people to God's service continues.

With reference to God holiness connotes both his separation from all that is human and earthly, and the distinct ethical aspects of his nature. The latter is seen in such passages as Leviticus 11:44; Isaiah 6:3,5; and Psalm 24:3-4. Jehovah is called "the Holy One" (Isa. 29:23; 40:25; 43:15).

In the Old Testament "holiness" was attributed to any place where God revealed himself or dwelt (Exod. 3:5; 28:29). All things used in the worship of Jehovah were holy (Exod. 29:33; 30:25; Lev. 16:4; 1 Kings 8:4). Because the Sabbath is related to Jehovah it is called "holy" (Exod. 20:8-11). Because Israel is the people of God they are to be holy as he is holy (Lev. 19:2).

In the New Testament the word "holy" is applied more to people than to things. (But see Matt. 4:5; Luke 1:72; Rom. 1:2; 2 Pet. 1:18). Holiness is to be more than outward ceremonial cleanness (Matt. 15:17-20). Other than in quotations from the Old Testament "holy" is not applied to God apart from the writings of John (John 17:11; Rev. 4:8; 6:10). But it is repeatedly used of the Spirit of God. It is also applied to Christ (e.g. Mark 1:24; Acts 3:14; Heb. 7:26).

In the New Testament all believers are called "saints" or "holy ones" (e.g. 1 Cor. 1:1; 2 Cor. 1:1). Though they did not always act saintly, they are holy in that they are set apart to God's service. 1 Peter 2:9 calls Christians "an holy nation." They are the new Israel of God set apart for his service. See *True Israel.*

Both the individual Christian and the churches are holy in that they are the "temple" or Holy of Holies of the Spirit of God (1 Cor. 3:16; 6:19). In the Hebrew tabernacle and Temple there were the *Holy Place* where sacrifices were made, and the *Holy of Holies* (see *Veil*) where God dwelt with his people in mercy. Now he dwells in his people and church.

The New Testament does not teach a progressive growth into the state of holiness or sinless perfection. The Christian is holy or sanctified by the indwelling of the Holy Spirit (John 14:17). But, of course, one should grow in ethical quality and service in the state of holiness. See *Baptism of the Holy Spirit.*

Holy of Holies; Holy Place. The "Holy Place" in the Hebrew tabernacle (Temple) was the place where the sacrifices were made. The "Holy of Holies" was a cube-shaped area behind the veil (see *Veil*) where God was said to dwell with his people in mercy. Exodus 26:33 calls them the "holy place" and the "most holy." Priests ministered daily in the Holy Place. But only the high priest might enter the Holy of Holies annually on the *Day of Atonement* (which see). In the Holy Place were the sacrificial altar, altar of incense, a golden candlestick or lamps, and the table for shewbread. In the Holy of Holies were the mercy seat and the ark of the covenant in which were placed the two tables of stone on which were written the Ten Commandments, a pot of manna, and Aaron's rod which budded (Heb. 9:1-5).

In Hebrews 9 the Holy Place is likened to Christ's earthly ministry including his death; the Holy of Holies is heaven itself where he appears before God with the evidence of his atoning work. Thus he is both the true Sacrifice and the High Priest (see Heb. 10:1-13).

Holy Spirit. The word for "Spirit" in both Testaments means wind, breeze, or breath. The verb form means to blow or breathe. The idea is an invisible power. The word "Holy" came to be used of the Spirit as denoting the moral and ethical qualities of God's character (Neh. 9:20; Psalm 51:11; Isa. 63:10). The idea in Spirit is the invisible power of God. In the Bible the Holy Spirit is always associated with power: physical, moral, ethical, spiritual. He is the Spirit of God sent forth to do his work. He is present in both Testaments, but is more prominent in the New Testament. The Holy Spirit is a person, one manifestation of the Godhead: Father, Son, and Spirit. He is called both "the Spirit of God" and "the Spirit of Christ" (Rom. 8:9).

In the Old Testament the Spirit is seen as active in creation (Gen. 1:2; Job 26:13; 33:4; Psalm 104:28-30). He is seen as coming upon individuals to enable them to do God's work (Exod. 35:30-35; Judges 3:10; 6:34; 13:25; 14:6). He enabled men to prophesy (Ezek. 2:2; Micah 3:8). He is related to the work of the Messiah (Isa. 61:1-3; see Luke 4:18-19). Joel 2:28 foretells the coming of the Spirit at Pentecost (Acts 2:16-21).

In the New Testament the work of the Holy Spirit is intimately related to the life and work of Jesus. He was the conceiving power in Jesus' virgin birth (Matt. 1:18,20; Luke 1:35). He came upon Jesus in fulness at his baptism (Matt. 3:16; Mark 1:10; Luke 3:22). Jesus worked no miracle until after this event. The Spirit led (Mark 1:12, "driveth") him into and during his wilderness temptation (Matt. 4:1; Luke 4:1). He worked in the power of the Spirit (Luke 4:18-19). He went to the cross "through the eternal Spirit" (Heb. 9:14). And he was raised from the dead "according to the spirit [Spirit] of holiness" (Rom. 1:4).

On the night before his death Jesus promised the Spirit to his disciples as "another [of the same kind] Comforter" or Helper (John 14:16) who would abide forever. (He has been called "Jesus' other self" [Marcus Dods] and "the other Jesus" [B. H. Carroll].) He would be their teacher and guide in understanding truth (John 14:26; 16:13). The Spirit will glorify Jesus, not himself (John 16:14). Thus it may be concluded that any system of religion or theology which magnifies the Holy Spirit above Jesus is not of the Holy Spirit (see 1 John 4:1).

The Holy Spirit convicts the world of sin, righteousness, and judgment (John 16:8-11; see *Conviction*). He effects the new birth (John 3:5,8). And at regeneration he indwells every Christian (John 14:17; see 1 Cor. 6:19). He baptizes the believer into the fellowship of believers (1 Cor. 12:13). He also indwells the church (1 Cor. 3:16). And his presence in the Christian is God's seal of ownership and guarantee that he will keep him saved (Eph. 1:13-14; see *Security of the Believer*).

At Pentecost the Spirit came in power upon the church (see *Pentecost*) to carry on the work which Jesus began (Acts 1:1). He empowers the church for witness (Acts 1:8); every new development in Acts in the spread of the gospel was by the command or with the approval of the Holy Spirit (Acts 8:15,26; 10:3,19,44; 11:12,15-16; 11:21,24; 13:2; 15:28; 16:6). The Holy Spirit is the administrator of the Godhead in missions—then and now.

The Holy Spirit inspired the writing of the Scriptures (2 Tim. 2:16; 2 Pet. 1:21; see *Revelation: Inspiration, Illumination*). And he bestows spiritual gifts upon Christians to enable them to do the Lord's work (1 Cor. 12). See *God; Jesus Christ; Unpardonable Sin*.

Hypocrisy, Hypocrite. The Greek word for "hypocrisy" means "acting a part" as in a drama. "Hypocrite" means one who does this. In the New Testament the former appears seven times (Matt. 23:28; 12:15; 12:1; 1 Tim. 4:2; 1 Pet. 2:1). It is rendered "dissimulation" in Galatians 2:13 and "condemnation" in James 5:12. The latter appears only in the Gospels and was used only by Jesus. He never used it of overt sinners, but only of those who appeared outwardly righteous but were inwardly unrighteous. Note his use of it concerning the Pharisees (Matt. 23). In this chapter Jesus uttered the harshest words ever to fall from his lips. Men should avoid this spiritual sin. And they should not use it of others. Only he who knows the inner man is qualified to do so.

Idolatry. This word means the worship of idols. The Old Testament forbade even the worship of Jehovah through visible symbols (Hos. 8:5-6; 10:5; see Exod. 20:4). In the New Testament idolatry not only refers to the worship of idols, but to giving any human desire first place above God and his will (Matt. 6:24; 1 Cor. 10:14; Gal. 5:20; Col. 3:5; 1 Pet. 4:3). Colossians 3:5 calls "covetousness" (the desire for more) idolatry. See *Covetousness*.

Immaculate Conception. This is often confused with Jesus' virgin birth. Actually this is a dogma of the Roman Catholic Church which says that the virgin Mary from the time of her own conception was "preserved free from all stain of original sin." This was proclaimed by Pope Pius X, December 8, 1854, but it has no support whatever in the New Testament.

Immortality. Immortality is more than the survival of the soul after the body dies. It involves the full life in heaven which includes both the soul and the resurrected body. This assurance is based upon man being made in God's image (Gen. 1:27). He is more than an animal. Of course, immortality in the above sense refers to the Christian. The lost live on eternally but in hell. Both saved and lost will be resurrected, but their end is different (John 5:29; see Luke 16:19-31).

Jesus' own resurrection is the guarantee of that of his people (John 14:19; 1 Cor. 15:20,23). First Thessalonians 4:13-17 assures believers who die before Jesus' return as well as those alive at that time of being ever with him. First Corinthians 15:51-57 gives details as to how the mortal and corruptible bodies become immortal and incorruptible. Peter says that believers have "a living hope" through Christ's resurrection of "an inheritance incorruptible and undefiled, and that fadeth not away, reserved in heaven" for them (1 Pet. 1:3-5; see 2 Tim. 1:10). See *Resurrection; Salvation.*

Inspiration. See *Revelation, Inspiration, Illumination.*

Intercession. Coming from the Latin *intercedo,* "to come between," this word translates both Hebrew and Greek words meaning to intercede or pray on behalf of another (Jer. 7:16; Rom. 8:26; 1 Tim. 2:1). Moses interceded for Israel (Exod. 32:11-13,31-32).

Jesus in his high priestly office made/makes intercession for his people (John 17; 1 John 2:2). Hebrews 9:11-28 presents Christ's atoning work as an intercession for man before God. "He ever liveth to make intercession for [on behalf of] them" (Heb. 7:25).

One of the most beautiful views of intercession is found in Romans 8:26-27. "Helpeth" means to stand over against another and help him lift his load (Luke 10:40). Sometimes one's prayer is so heavy he cannot lift it up to God. It is then that the Holy Spirit helps to lift it. He "maketh intercession for us with groanings which cannot be uttered" or with sighs too deep for words. Thus by the Holy Spirit's intercession a groan in one's soul may be in God's ears the most eloquent of prayers. See *Prayer*.

Intermediate State. This refers to the interval between one's death and the final resurrection. It is not a time of soul sleeping or an unconscious state (Matt. 17:3; 22:31-32; Rev. 7:9-17).

In the story of the rich man and Lazarus (Luke 16:22-26) both died. But Lazarus is seen at the heavenly banquet leaning on Abraham's bosom, the place of greatest honor. The rich man is in hell enduring torment. Note the shift in conditions between this life and the afterlife. Since the rich man is conscious, it follows that Lazarus is also. So at death the righteous enter heaven with its joys; the unrighteous enter hell with its suffering. At the Lord's return both will be raised in their resurrection bodies to appear before the judgment seat of Christ (Rom. 14:10; 2 Cor. 5:10; see John 5:29). It is evident that this appearance will not determine whether or not one is saved or lost; it will be with respect to degrees of reward in heaven and punishment in hell (see *Judgment, Last*).

The New Testament speaks largely from the standpoint of the Christian. But we catch a glimpse through the veil as to all who die before the Lord's return. Certainly Christians are now with him (1 Thess. 4:14).

Jealousy. In both Testaments the words for "jealousy" carry the idea of heat or warmth. The Greek word is the one whence comes "zeal." Jealousy is used in both the bad and good sense. Jehovah's jealousy is a good sense based upon his love. He regards Israel as his wife, and idolatry is seen as spiritual adultery (Deut. 32:16,21).

In the good sense when jealousy is attributed to men it is zeal for God's honor (2 Cor. 11:2; note "zeal" in Rom. 10:2). In the evil sense "jealousy" rendered as "envy" (KJV) is seen in Acts 7:9 (cf. Rom. 13:13; 1 Cor. 3:3, 2 Cor. 12:20; James 3:14,16).

Jehovah. This is the name of the true God of Israel. It is formed from the Hebrew verb "to be" (Exod. 3:13-15). The Hebrew form is *Yahweh*. In the Old Testament (KJV) it is translated "Lord" (Gen. 2:4; Psalm 23:1). See *God; Jesus Christ*.

Jerusalem, The New. The term "new Jerusalem" appears only in Revelation 21:2. It is called the "holy city . . . coming down from God out of heaven, prepared as a bride adorned [cosmetized] for her husband." This last phrase suggests that it is the people of God as the "bride" with Christ as the Bridegroom. Chapter 21 describes this city in highly symbolic language. One may imagine chapter 22 as descriptive of the inside of this city. It is a picture patterned after Eden before man's fall. The term "holy city" is drawn from the fact that the earthly Jerusalem was the holy city of the Jews. This seems to be one symbol of heaven with God's people in perfect fellowship and bliss. See Galatians 4:26; Hebrews 11:10; 12:22.

Jesus Christ. Jesus Christ is the Son of God, the Savior of the world and both Lord and Head of the church (Col. 1:18). Of him Ralph Waldo Emerson said, "The name of Jesus is not so much written as plowed into the history of the world." He is the full revelation of God as Redeemer (Heb. 1:1-3); his work is the key to the understanding of history (Rev. 5).

The Bible accords many names to him: such as seed of the woman (Gen. 3:15); true "seed" of Abraham (Gal. 3:16); Branch of Jehovah (Isa. 4:2); Immanuel (Isa. 7:14; Matt. 1:23); Wonderful Counsellor, mighty God, everlasting Father, Prince of Peace (Isa. 9:6); servant of Jehovah (Isa. 42:1); Teacher or Rabbi (Matt. 8:19); Judge (John 5:27); Savior (Luke 2:11); son of David (Matt. 20:31); Lamb of God (John 1:29); second Adam (1 Cor. 15:45); root and offspring of David, and the bright and morning star (Rev. 22:16).

"Jesus" is the Greek equivalent of the Hebrew "Joshua" *(Yeshua)* meaning "Jehovah is salvation" (Matt. 1:21). It is the human, personal, saving name of the Lord meaning that the eternal God has come in flesh for man's salvation (Acts 4:12). "Christ" is his official title, the Greek equivalent of the Hebrew "Messiah," "Anointed One," which sums up the Jewish expectations of the "Coming One" (Luke 7:19). Since for Jesus' hearers this name carried a political-military meaning, except for one private discussion (John 4:25-26) and testimony under oath (Matt. 26:63-64), he never used this title for himself. The same is true of "son of David." But he did commend Peter for his confession of him as "the Christ, the son of the living God" (Matt. 16:16-17). The term "Christ" eventually came to be used as a personal name for him

(1 Cor. 15:3). It was a synonym for deity. "Lord" when used of Jesus in the purely Christian sense means that Jesus Christ is God in flesh for man's salvation (Rom. 1:3; 10:9; 1 Cor. 11:23).

Worthy of note is the name "Word" or *Logos* used only by John to refer to Jesus Christ (John 1:1,14; 1 John 1:1; 5:7; Rev. 19:13). A common word in Greek writings, John's use of the term is most likely Hebrew in meaning. Some see it related to the Hebrew *memra,* word, or the wisdom of Jehovah (Prov. 8). It means an open spoken manifestation of God. John's "in the beginning" (1:1) suggests Genesis 1:1. Each new phase of creation begins with "And God said" (Gen. 1:3,6,9,11,14,20,24,26)—God's spoken word or open manifestation. This is probably John's source of "Word."

Jesus' favorite self-identification is "Son of man" (cf. Matt. 8:2; 16:13; Mark 10:33; Luke 19:10; John 3:14). It identifies him with man, and probably is related to Daniel 7:13. After the Gospels it appears only in Acts 7:56; Revelation 1:13.

Of course, Jesus is called "Son of God" (Luke 1:32). He often used it of himself (cf. Matt. 11:27; John 3:16-17; see John 10:30). Peter used it of him (Matt. 16:16). But in direct address to Jesus this title and its cognates were used only by demons (cf. Mark 5:7; Luke 4:41). Under oath Jesus admitted that he was the Son of God (Matt. 26:63-64).

John 1:1 declares the eternity of Christ. Literally, "In the beginning always was the Word [Christ], and the Word always was equal with God, and the Word always was God himself." He is coeternal, coequal, and coexistent with God the Father. And he is the intermediate Agent of the Godhead in creation (John 1:3; Col. 1:16; Heb. 1:2). In his redemptive work he is re-creating all things (2 Cor. 5:17; Rev. 21:5). And he is the cohesive force sustaining the universe (Col. 1:17). The universe is not heliocentric but Christocentric; it centers not in the *sun* but in the *Son.*

This eternal Christ became flesh as Jesus of Nazareth (John 1:14,17), the full revelation of God as redeeming love (John 1:16-18). He was born of a virgin (Matt. 1:18-25; Luke 1:26-38; 2:1-20). Conceived of the Holy Spirit, he is God. Born of the virgin Mary, he is man—he is Deity-Humanity, the God-Man. Because he partakes of the nature of both, God and man meet in him in reconciliation (1 Tim. 2:5-6; see *Mediator*).

Tempted in all things like as men are, yet without sin, he is the perfect Sacrifice for man's sin (Matt. 4:1-11; Luke 4:1-13; Heb. 4:15-16). Someone said that Jesus' sinless life in a corrupt world is as great a moral miracle as his virgin birth is a biological miracle. Though sinless, he was made sin for man, that in him man might have the righteousness of God (2 Cor. 5:21).

Jesus died on a cross as man's substitute. He was raised bodily from death for man's justification (Matt. 27:33-35; 28:1-8; Rom. 1:4; 4:25). After a series of ten appearances to his disciples over a period of forty days, he ascended to the Father (Acts 1:9). Seated at God's right hand he is now reigning in his mediatorial kingdom (1 Cor. 15:25-28; Heb. 10:12-13), where he holds intercession for his people (Heb. 7:25; 1 John 2:1). And he is coming again at the end of the age to receive his own who will be with him forever in glory (Matt. 24:27,30-31,42-47; Acts 1:11; 1 Thess: 4:13-18; Titus 2:13; Heb. 9:28).

Revelation presents the final triumph of Christ over all his enemies (11:15; 19:11-21). See *Judgment; Temptation.*

Jesus Christ, Trial of. The trial of Jesus consisted of two parts (Jewish and Roman), and each of these contained three parts: Jewish (before Annas, John 18:12-14,19-23; before the Sanhedrin before dawn, Matt. 26:57,59-68; and after dawn, Luke 22:66-71); Roman (before Pilate the former time, John 18:28-38; before Herod Antipas, Luke 23:6-12; before Pilate again, Matt. 27:15-26; John 18:39 to 19:16). Since Rome reserved to itself capital punishment, the Sanhedrin had to turn him over to Pilate, the Roman procurator.

The trials were illegal in every sense. The Sanhedrin's decision to kill Jesus was made weeks before his arrest (John 11:47-53). Jewish law required trials only in daytime; Jesus' first two were at night. Those who perpetrated his arrest also sat as the judges. The high priest was supposed to protect the prisoner's interests; Caiaphas browbeat Jesus as he led in the prosecution. A prisoner was not to be abused physically; temple police did this to Jesus. False witnesses were used. Jesus was convicted on his own testimony. In capital cases a day must intervene between conviction and sentence. This was not done. The Sanhedrin convicted Jesus of blasphemy (Mark 14:64), but before Pilate they accused him of insurrection (Luke 23:2).

Herod Antipas made a mockery of the whole thing (Luke 23:6-12). While Pilate went through normal court procedure, three times he declared Jesus innocent of any crime (Luke 23:4,14-15,22). Yet to placate the Jews and save his own skin (John 19:12-13), he had Jesus scourged and then turned him over to soldiers to be crucified. Never in all history has there been so great a miscarriage of justice. Men thought/think Jesus was/is on trial before them, when all the while they were/are on trial before him.

Joy. The element of joy is prominent in both Testaments. Note the Psalms. But its fullest expression is found in the New Testament. The Greek words used most often are related to the word for "grace." Joy is more than *happiness* which suggests its relation to *happenings*. It is the inner emotion of rejoicing in spite of outward circumstances—somewhat like peace. In the shadow of the cross Jesus spoke of his joy (John 15:11; 17:13). When his people are persecuted they are to rejoice or exult, shout for joy (Matt. 5:12). Paul speaks of joy as one fruit of the Spirit (Gal. 5:22). Such a joy is related to faith (Phil. 1:25) and hope (Rom. 5:2). Joy is the theme of Philippians—even though Paul dictated it while in prison.

Such a joy knows no gloom or defeatism. It is more than gaiety or whistling in the dark. It comes from the assurance that despite outward circumstances one is safe and triumphant in the Lord. It sees through the present suffering to the ultimate goal (Heb. 12:2).

Judas Iscariot. Judas Iscariot will ever remain a mystery. But he stands as a lesson and warning to all who propose to follow Jesus.

"Judas" is the Greek form of the Hebrew "Judah." Judas Maccabaeus was the great Jewish hero in the interbiblical period. One of Jesus' half-brothers (Jude) bore this name. "Iscariot" means a "man of Kerioth," a village probably in Southern Judea. So his name and village suggest that he was of the tribe of Judah, the tribe whence came Jesus. How different these descendants of Judah were. One exalted his name to glory; the other brought it down to the deepest shame.

The first scriptural reference to Judas is in the list of the apostles (Matt. 10:4; Mark 3:19; Luke 6:16). With one accord these Gospels cite him as the betrayer of Jesus. John's first mention of him sounds the same dreadful note (6:71). He was the only apostle from Judea.

Four views have been set forth about Judas' act. (1) Judas was foreordained to be the traitor. John 6:64 says that Jesus knew from the beginning who would betray him. But foreknowledge of an event does not necessarily cause it. That Judas was not a puppet is evidenced by Jesus' words of woe about the betrayer (Luke 22:22). This position hardly coincides with the character of God. (2) That Judas was a superpatriot. He felt that Jesus' movement would bring revolution that would destroy his nation. (3) That he was a super-Christian who sought to force Jesus to declare his Messiahship. His bargain to betray Jesus for a price argues against (2) and (3). (4) That his betrayal came as the climax to a gradual development. This seems to fit the evidence.

Judas was beset with avaricious ambition. He probably followed Jesus expecting to receive a prominent place in his kingdom. Why did Jesus choose him as an apostle? Could it be that he saw in him abilities which if dedicated to him would be an asset in the Christian movement? But Judas never dedicated himself to Jesus. While the others called Jesus "Lord," Judas never did (Matt. 26:21-25). He called him "Master," meaning teacher or rabbi.

One year before the betrayal, Jesus saw evidences in Judas tending toward that end (John 6:70). Note "one of you is [not 'was'] a devil." When finally he saw that Jesus would die (Matt. 26:2), he sought to get what he could out of it. Seeing that he could not get his thieving hands on the money derived from the sale of Mary's ointment (about fifty-two dollars, John 12:4-6), he bargained to betray him for thirty pieces of silver (about twenty-five dollars), the price of a slave (Matt. 26:15; Zech. 11:12). It was only a matter of hours until Satan took him over completely (John 13:23-30), and he went forth with *night* in his soul to perform his terrible deed (Matt. 26:48-49).

The word for Judas' repentance means simply regret, not a change of attitude, heart, and mind (Matt. 27:3). He reached for so much, and got nothing but lasting infamy and a lost soul.

Judgment, Last. This event will herald the end of the age. Some interpreters see a judgment of the nations based on how they have treated the Jews (Matt. 25:31-46), as well as the White Throne Judgment (Rev. 20:11-15). However, it seems that nations are judged within the context of history. The writer sees these as two facets of the one final judgment.

Note that all men appear before God as the Judge (Rev. 20:12). Paul sees Christ also involved in this judgment (2 Cor. 5:10). But, of course, Christ is the manifestation of God. This judgment will not determine who is saved or lost, only declare it. It will be a judgment "out of those things which are written in the books, according to their works" (v. 12). It will determine the degree of rewards in heaven (Matt. 25:14-23) or of punishment in hell (Luke 12:47-48). All whose names appear in the "book of life" will be forever with the Lord in heaven; all others will be cast into the lake of fire (hell, v. 15). "This is the second death" (v. 14) or eternal separation from God.

Justification. This is an act of God in which he declares believers as justified or righteous before him. This doctrine is at the heart of Paul's writings, but is also set forth throughout the New Testament. It is centered in the fact of man's sinfulness and God's gracious act of atonement wrought in Jesus Christ (Rom. 3:23-26). It is based not upon man's legal obedience but upon God's grace through man's faith (Rom. 3:20-22; Eph. 2:8-10). Justification does not mean that God ignores sin, but that he has provided in Christ grounds in keeping with his holy righteous nature whereby he may judicially declare believers as justified in his sight (Rom. 4:25). It does not mean that the Christian is fully just, but that God chooses to regard him as such in Christ. See *Righteousness*.

Kenosis. This word refers to the doctrine expressed in Philippians 2:7 where "made himself of no reputation" renders the Greek phrase "emptied himself" (*ekenōsen*, Greek, "emptied."). Debates have raged as to what Christ emptied in his incarnation. Certainly not of his deity (John 10:30; Col. 2:9). What Christ did was to empty himself from one *form* into another, such as pouring water from a round into a square glass without losing any water. His true self remained the same, but the outward appearance assumed the role of humanity apart from sin. He was Deity-Humanity or the God-Man in his incarnation.

In his humanity he assumed the lowest role of men, that of a slave. The Gospel record shows that he took on certain human limitations. He had to learn as a child (Luke 2:52). He grew weary, and experienced amazement (Matt. 8:10). Though wiser than any other man, he expressed limitation of knowledge as to the time of his second coming (Mark 13:32). He spoke what his Father told him, and he had not spoken of that (John 8:26; Acts 1:7). E. Y. Mullins likens these limitations to Paderewski playing the piano while wearing gloves. It was a voluntary limitation which is an expression, not of weakness, but of power.

Since Christ became obedient to the most painful and shameful of deaths, the Father exalted him above his former glory, from that of Creator to that of Creator-Redeemer (Phil. 9). Before him every knee shall bow and every tongue shall confess that "Jesus Christ is Lord, to the glory of God the Father" (Phil. 2:10-11). See *Glory* and *Jesus Christ.*

Kingdom of God (of Heaven), The. The Greek word for "kingdom" may also read "sovereignty." In its broader sense it refers to God's sovereign rule in his universe. But in the strictly spiritual sense it connotes his rule in men's hearts (Matt. 6:10; Luke 17:20-21).

Some interpreters distinguish between the "kingdom of God" and the "kingdom of heaven." But a comparison of the Gospels shows that the terms are used interchangeably (cf. Matt. 13:11; Mark 4:11).

Satan made a false claim to sovereignty in the universe (Luke 4:5-7). The purpose of Christ's incarnation was to prove this claim false. This was accomplished in his death and resurrection. The climax of Revelation is found in 11:15. Literally, "The sovereignty of the cosmos became that of our Lord [Jehovah] and of his Christ, and he shall reign [as sovereign] unto the ages of the ages."

Lake of Fire. This figure is found only in Revelation 19:20;

20:14-15 (see Rev. 21:8). This is the place into which are finally consigned the beast, false prophet, the devil, and unredeemed people (cf. Luke 16:23-24). This is a figure of hell as the place of everlasting punishment. That it does not mean annihilation is seen in "for ever and ever" (Greek, "unto the *everlasting*). The figure of "fire and brimstone" suggests Genesis 19:24 at the destruction of Sodom and Gomorrah. There it "rained" down. Here it is collected in a lake, suggesting the totality of punishment. See *Gehenna; Hell.*

Lamb of God. This is the title bestowed upon Jesus by John the Baptist (John 1:29-36; see Isa. 53:7). This term reminds one of the place of the lamb in Hebrew sacrifice, especially the paschal lamb (Exod. 12:21). Jesus is referred to as a lamb in Revelation twenty-eight times. "A Lamb as it had been slain" (Rev. 5:6) means one with its throat cut, the usual method of slaying a lamb for sacrifice. So Jesus as "the Lamb of God" shows his atoning death by which the sin of the world is taken or borne away. He bore man's sin as if it were his own (Isa. 53:5). See 1 Peter 1:19.

Lasciviousness. This word expresses an utter lack of morals. It is so translated six times in the New Testament (Mark 7:22; 2 Cor. 12:21; Gal. 5:19; Eph. 4:19; 1 Pet. 4:3; Jude 4). It is rendered as "wantonness" in Romans 13:13 and 2 Peter 2:18, and as "filthy" in 2 Peter 2:7.

Last Judgment. See *Judgment.*

Last Time, Times. This term is found in 1 Peter 1:5; 1:20 (plural); 1 John 2:18; Jude 18. First John 2:18 reads, literally, "the last hour." The Old Testament regarded this idea as including the entire period of the Messianic revelation. In this sense the New Testament usage may be regarded as the time extending from the birth or resurrection of Christ to the end of the age—that is, when spoken of as being present (e.g. 1 John 2:18). However, the usage in 1 Peter 1:5 definitely looks to the end of the age.

Life. The Greek words so translated mean life in its various aspects. One word whence comes "biology" *(bios)* refers to life in its physical aspects. Five times it is rendered "life" (Luke 8:14; 1 Tim. 2:2; 2 Tim. 2:4; 1 Pet. 4:3; 1 John 2:16); five times it is translated "living" (Mark 12:44; Luke 8:43; 15:12,30; 21:4); once it means "good" in the sense of things necessary for physical life (1 John 3:17).

Another word whence comes "psychology" *(psuchē)* is used one hundred and five times. Its principal uses are "soul" (Matt. 10:28) and "life" (Luke 6:9). It may refer to the animal principle of life, the spiritual self, or the purpose of living. All these meanings may be seen in Matthew 16:25-26.

The word most often used (134 times) is one whence comes the word "zoology" *(zoē).* Only once is it used for other than "life" ("lifetime," Luke 16:25). This word usually refers to spiritual life or life from God through Christ (John 3:16; 10:10). This kind of life is the main theme of the New Testament. Even when the idea of natural life is present, it is colored by God's enrichment of life (Luke 1:75). This kind of life is especially presented in John's Gospel (used thirty-six times). *Bios* is not used in this Gospel; *psuchē* is translated "life" eight times (10:11,15,17; 12:25; 13:37-38; 15:13), otherwise it renders *zoē*.

"In him was life; and the life was the light of men" (John 1:4). "I am the way, the truth, and the life: no man cometh unto the Father, but by me" (John 14:6).

Light. This word is used in the Bible in the sense of both natural (Gen. 1:14-18) and artificial light, such as from lamps (Acts 20:8). But it most often connotes mental, moral, and spiritual light. The last use is that of light in the sense of good as opposed to darkness as evil (1 John 1:5). Jesus is the Light of the world (John 1:9; 8:12; Luke 2:32). Christians are called the light of the world as they reflect the light that is in Christ (Matt. 5:14,16; Eph. 5:14).

Logos. This Greek word is translated as "word." From it comes the English word "logic." In classical Greek it is used as "reason" and "word." Though used in the Bible mostly as "word," this usage also implies reason. The philosophers used it to denote such ideas as the soul of the world (Stoics) and the generative process in nature (Marcus Aurelius). Philo, the Jewish-Alexandrian philosopher-theologian used it about thirteen hundred times, at times almost as a person. It appears in the New Testament three hundred and thirty times, two hundred and eighteen as "word."

John used it seven times to refer to Christ as a person (John

1:1,14; 1 John 1:1; 5:7; Rev. 19:13). Some hold that his source of this use is Grecian. The discovery of the Dead Sea scrolls shows the thought patterns of John to be those of the first century prior to A.D. 70. So John's source of the word for Christ is Hebraic. Some interpreters trace it to the Hebrew word for "word." Others see it as reflecting "wisdom" in Proverbs 8. Basically *logos* connotes an open, spoken manifestation of the speaker. Since John began his Gospel with "in the beginning" it suggests his source of "Logos" as "and God said" which introduces each new phase of God's creative work (Gen. 1:3,6,9,11,14,20,24,26,29; see John 1:3; Col. 1:15-17; Heb. 1:2-3). See *Jesus Christ.*

Longsuffering; Kindness. These words belong to the same school of thought in progressive fashion. "Longsuffering" renders a Greek word which means long of mind or soul. It expresses the quality of suffering long injury before striking back. Used of God it means forbearing sinners and slowness to execute judgment, not out of indifference toward sin but of love for the sinner (Rom. 2:4; 2 Pet. 3:9). It is a part of the fruit of the Spirit (Gal. 5:22). Thus it is an attitude which Christians should show toward others (Eph. 4:2; Col. 3:12).

"Kindness" goes one step further. It connotes the attitude of one who seeks to do good to one who has harmed him, or returning good for evil (2 Cor. 6:6; Eph. 2:7; Col. 3:12). Note that it is joined with "longsuffering" in Colossians 3:12. Also in Galatians 5:22 where the Greek word for kindness is translated "gentleness" (KJV); in the Revised Version it reads "kindness." Thus both of these virtues are parts of "the fruit of the Spirit." The verb forms of both words appear in 1 Corinthians 13:4 as qualities of Christian love *(agapē).*

Lord; The Lord. "Lord" translates the Greek word *kurios* which appears seven hundred and forty-nine times in the New Testament. It means variously owner or master (Matt. 15:27b), sir (John 4:11; Acts 16:30); "Lord" in Acts 9:5 probably should read "sir," but note "Lord" twice in verse 6. The word is rendered "Lord" six hundred and sixty-seven times. When used of Jesus in the strictly Christian sense it means Jehovah in flesh (see John 20:28 where it is joined with "God"; "Lord" translates "Jehovah" or *Yahweh* in the Old Testament KJV). Another Greek word (*despotēs*, note "despot") is rendered "Lord" five times (Luke 2:29; Acts 4:24; 2 Pet. 2:1; Jude 4; Rev. 6:10). Luke uses another word (*epistatēs*, the captain of a ship) in the sense of "Lord" (see "Master" in 5:5; 8:24,45; 9:33,49; 17:13).

When used of Jesus one clearly sees the lordship of Jesus Christ. The Christian can make no greater confession than that "Jesus is Lord" and then live it (Rom. 10:10; 1 Cor. 12:3). In Philippians 2:11 Paul foresees the time when all "in heaven . . . earth . . . and under the earth" [hell?]" will confess "that Jesus Christ is Lord, to the glory of God the Father." Those in heaven gladly will do so. Those on earth should. Ultimately by the power of God's might those in hell will confess that he whom they rejected truly is the Lord—but for them it will be everlastingly too late! See Revelation 19:16. See *Jesus Christ*.

Lord's Day. "Lord's Day" occurs in the New Testament only in Revelation 1:10. But it is used in early Christian nonbiblical literature. Ignatius wrote, "No longer keeping the Sabbath but live according to the Lord's day, on which also our Light arose." *The Gospel of Peter* used such phrases as "The Lord's day began to dawn" and "early on the Lord's day" (cf. Matt. 28:1; Luke 24:1). Another writer using the name of Barnabas says that Christians used the "eighth day with gladness," the day on which Jesus rose from the dead.

The word rendered "Lord's" is an adjective, "Lordly" (cf. 1 Cor. 11:20). It means "belonging to the lord" or "Lord." At one time thought to be a purely Christian word, archaeological discoveries show it to have been in common use to refer to days dedicated to Caesar. In protest to this the Christians used it to refer to the Lord's resurrection day. It probably was used as a protest against emperor worship. Days dedicated to this were called "the Augustean day." Hence the significance of "the Lord's day" in Revelation 1:10.

This day was obviously the first day of the week (Matt. 28:1). Some Christians still insist upon observing the seventh day as one of worship. However, "Sabbath" means "rest" not "seventh." The Sabbath commemorated God's *resting* from his creative work (Gen.

2:2-3; Exod. 20:8-11). On the first day of the week God *rested* from his redemptive work in Christ. Hence its use by Christians as their day of special worship. Jesus observed the seventh day (prior to his resurrection), but he appeared to his disciples *after* his resurrection on the first day of the week (John 20:19-29). Paul told the Corinthians to lay by in store their gifts "upon the first day of the week," the day they assembled for worship (1 Cor. 16:2). Where Christians *as Christians* assembled for worship it was on the first day of the week (Acts 20:7). The seventh day is a day of *commemoration;* the first day is one of *celebration.*

Lord's Supper. This is the name given to one of two ordinances in a New Testament church, *baptism* (which see) being the other. In the New Testament order it is preceded by baptism (Acts 2:41-42). The accounts of its beginning are recorded in Matthew 26:26-29; Mark 14:22-25; Luke 22:14-20; 1 Corinthians 11:23-26; see also 1 Cor. 10:16-17.

Like baptism the Lord's Supper is not a sacrament (necessary for salvation). It is a symbol of what Jesus Christ did for man's salvation. The unleavened bread symbolizes his body; the "fruit of the vine" (Mark 14:25) symbolizes his "blood of the new testament [covenant] which is shed for many" (Mark 14:24). The ordinance also symbolizes the believer's faith in the second coming of Christ (Mark 14:25; 1 Cor. 11:26). Thus the Supper commemorates what Christ has done and will do with regard to man's salvation. See *Baptism.*

Love. Two basic Greek verbs in the New Testament are used to express love: *phileō,* to love in warm friendship (note Philadelphia, the city of brotherly love); and *agapaō,* to love with the highest kind of love. The former appears twenty-five times in the New Testament, twenty-two of which are rendered "love" (Mark 6:5; Luke 20:46; John 5:20; 11:3,36; 12:25; 15:19; 16:27; 20:2; 21:15-17; 1 Cor. 16:22; Titus 3:15; Rev. 3:19; 22:15). In classical Greek the former was used more often; the latter was regarded as a cold word. Perhaps this scarcity led to its being used more often in the New Testament (one hundred and forty-two times) to express the idea of the God-kind-of-love or Christian love (cf. Matt. 5:43-46; John 3:16). In his writings John used this word seventy-two times.

However, he also used both verbs to express Jesus' love (John 11:3,5). The basic meaning in *agapaō* is absolute loyalty to its object.

The noun form *agapē* is used one hundred and sixteen times, eighty-six times as "love." Another form of this word is used sixty-two times, forty-seven as "beloved." Thus one can see that the New Testament places the greater emphasis upon this kind of love.

Agapē is used for the very nature of God (1 John 4:8). It is the love which he demonstrated on the cross (Rom. 5:8). Christians are urged to love each other in the same fashion (John 15:12-13). This word is rendered as "charity" (KJV) in 1 Corinthians 13, which shows that this love should be the basis of all Christian actions. See *Hate.*

Lust. The word most often rendered "lust" basically means "desire." It can be in a good sense, as in both verb and noun in Luke 22:15. Or it can mean "lust" as in John 8:44. In each case the context must decide. In James 1:14-15 it is possible to see both uses. "His own lust" in verse 14 may mean one's natural desire; in verse 15 it is clearly "lust." God gives men certain desires for good if properly used (for instance, ambition, hunger, sex). Satan seeks to pervert these desires into lust.

Another word whence comes "hedonist" is used three times as "pleasure" (Luke 8:14; Titus 3:3; 2 Pet. 2:13), and "lust" in James 4:1,3. But all connote evil pleasures. Still another word means a strong craving (Rom. 1:11; 2 Cor. 5:2; 9:14; Phil. 1:8; 2:26; 1 Thess. 3:6; 2 Tim. 1:4; 1 Pet. 2:2). Only in James 4:5 does it have the evil sense. A word whence comes "pathos" is used meaning "passion." Without exception it is used in the evil sense (Rom. 1:26; Col. 3:5; 1 Thess. 4:5). Such a word study reminds one how carefully he should exercise the emotions and powers of his body. They should be surrendered to the Lord, not used as tools of Satan. See *Temptation.*

Magi, The. The word "magi" is translated "wise men" in Matthew 2:1,7,16. According to Herodotus originally this was a Median tribe which later became a tribe of priests. It is said that Zoroaster may have come from this tribe. Among other things they were students of astrology and astronomy. Probably they were familiar with Jewish Messianic expectations learned from Jewish priests who were in Babylonia during and following the Babylonian captivity.

According to the ancients the appearing of a new heavenly body heralded some intervention of God in history. Both Tacitus and Suetonius tell of a widespread belief in the East that at that time one starting from Judea would become a world ruler. When the Magi saw "his star" (Matt. 2:2) they naturally interpreted this as referring to such a person. So they journeyed to Jerusalem to the king's palace, asking, "Where is he that is born King of the Jews? for we have seen his star in the east [they saw it in the east country but it led them westward], and are come to worship him" (Matt. 2:2).

Tradition says that there were three of them, drawn from the number of gifts they brought (Matt. 2:11). But this is only speculation. These men, probably from Babylonia, heralded that multitude from all nations who eventually would come to receive Christ.

Mammon. This is the Aramaic word for riches or wealth. In the New Testament it is used only in Matthew 6:24; Luke 16:9,11,13. In the former Jesus says that one cannot be a slave to both God and Mammon. Both demand absolute loyalty which cannot be given to two persons or things.

In the parable of the unrighteous or *shrewd* steward some see Jesus as approving his acts (Luke 16:8), but this is merely a part of the story. His reference to "the mammon of unrighteousness" simply means that it is a tyrant if not properly controlled and used. The New Testament strongly warns against the abuse of wealth. Money is a great servant but a terrible master. One cannot serve both God and mammon, but he can serve God with mammon. See *Stewardship*.

Maranatha; Anathema. The former of these words is from two Aramaic words *maran atha*. This word means "Our Lord cometh" or "will come." Some see it as "has come." But probably the other ideas apply.

Anathema means "accursed" or set for destruction. These two words are used together in 1 Corinthians 16:22 *(anathema marana tha)*. In this sense the latter seems to be used to add a solemn emphasis to the former. But even here the emphasis seems to be that those not loving "the Lord" ("Jesus Christ" not in best manuscripts) should be accursed because or when the Lord comes.

Marketplace. In ancient times the marketplace *(agora)* was a busy center of life in a town or city (Matt. 11:16; Acts 17:17). The verb form means to buy (Matt. 13:44,46; John 6:5). A compound form meaning to buy out of the marketplace is rendered "redeeming" (Eph. 5:16). The marketplace was a place where children played (Luke 7:32), the unemployed waited for employment (Matt. 20:3), the proud paraded for public recognition (Matt. 20:7), trials were held (Acts 16:19), and men gathered for philosophical, political, and religious discussion (Acts 17:17). It was in the marketplace in Athens that Paul came to the attention of philosophers which led to his sermon on Mars' Hill (Acts 17:18-33). See *Babbler.*

Marriage. In Hebrew life the three great events in one's life were birth, marriage, and death, marriage being the greatest. The Talmud said, "Any Jew who has not a wife is no man."

Among the ancient Jews marriage consisted of betrothal and the wedding itself. A couple might be promised in infancy by their parents. When the girl reached marriageable age she could accept or reject the arrangement. If she accepted it, betrothal took place. This was more than our engagement but less than marriage. This period lasted for some time, perhaps a year. During this time sexual infidelity on the part of the girl was considered as adultery, and was punishable by death unless the man chose to put her away quietly. This entire custom is reflected in the case of Mary and Joseph (Matt. 1:18-25; Luke 1:26-38).

The Bible is vague about the exact nature of the marriage ceremony itself. Two things stand out: the marriage procession and the marriage feast. The procession was usually at night. The "friend of the bridegroom" (John 3:29) brought the bride and her attendants to the home of the bridegroom (cf. Matt. 9:15). The bridegroom was absent from his home at the time. After the bride was at his home he also came in a procession with his friends. The friend of the bridegroom rejoices to hear the bridegroom's voice upon his arrival, for then his work is done (cf. Rev. 18:23). John the

Baptist used this figure to show the relation of his ministry to that of Jesus.

The wedding feast was a prominent part of the marriage proceedings. To refuse an invitation to such was a grave insult (Matt. 22:1-10). Likewise if one were not invited. An ancient proverb said, "He who does not invite me to his marriage will not have me to his funeral." The marriage feast usually lasted for several days with different guests coming at appointed times (John 2:1-11).

Jesus often drew upon the figures of marriage to teach Christian truth (Matt. 9:15; 22:1-12; 25:1-13; see also Rev. 19:7-9; 21:2). See *Virgin Birth.*

Martyr. Strictly speaking a "martyr" was one who bore witness or firsthand testimony. The word is used also of those who died for their faith (Acts 22:20; Rev. 2:13; 17:6). Such gave witness with their death. See *Witness.*

Master. This word renders various Greek words: the one whence comes "despot" (1 Tim. 6:1-2; 2 Tim. 2:21; Titus 2:9; 1 Pet. 2:18; rendered "Lord" in Luke 2:29; Acts 4:24; 2 Pet. 2:1; Jude 4; Rev. 6:10); "Lord" as of God or Christ (Matt. 1:20,22,24; as "Master," Matt. 6:24; 15:27; Mark 13:35; Rom. 14:4); the word meaning "leader" rendered "Master" (Matt. 23:8,10); Greek word *didaskalos* or Hebrew *Rabbi* (Matt. 8:19; Mark 4:38; Matt. 26:25,49). These are but a few of many examples. See *Lord.*

Mediator; Mediation. In the Old Testament mediation is seen in various aspects: that or those who were designed to bring God and man together. These include God communicating with man through prophets and the office of king and priest. The Old Testament sacrificial system was a form of mediation. The same is seen in intercessory prayer (Gen. 18:22-33; Exod. 32:30-32). In Job 9:33 the patriarch wished for a "daysman" or mediator between him and God. In Isaiah the Suffering Servant is the climax of mediation in the Old Testament: God's messenger to man (42:6,19; 43:10; 49:2; 50:4-5; 61:1-3). In Isaiah 53 he is the sacrifice to bring man to God (note especially verses 4-6,12).

In the New Testament Christ is Prophet (Matt. 13:57), Priest (Heb. 5:1-10), and King (Matt. 25:31; 28:18). Note his high priestly intercessory prayer in John 17. The epistle to the Hebrews presents him as superior to all Old Testament means of mediation. First John 2:1 presents him as the Christian's "advocate" before the Father. First Corinthians 15:25-28 sees him reigning in his mediatorial kingdom to bring both believing men and nature into harmony with God's will (cf. Eph. 2:11-22; Col. 1:13-14,20-22).

The word "mediator" appears in the New Testament only in 1 Timothy 2:5. Such was one appointed to bring two estranged parties together. He must perfectly represent both, and do all necessary to effect a reconciliation. As the God-Man (partaking of the nature of both) Christ Jesus did this; in him both God and man meet in reconciliation. See 2 Corinthians 5:19-21. As the Mediator Christ Jesus effected mediation through his death and resurrection. See *Atonement; Prayer; Salvation.*

Meekness. This word was looked down upon by pagan Greeks. But the Holy Spirit has made it one of the highest Christian graces (Gal. 5:23). It is the spirit of Jesus himself (Matt. 11:29; cf. 2 Cor. 10:1). He said, "Blessed are the meek: for they shall inherit the earth" (Matt. 5:5).

Basically the word means one who is teachable. It is the opposite of a know-it-all. In secular writings it was used of a horse that had been broken to ride or work. One did not break his spirit or strength, but brought them under control for effective use. This is what the Lord wants in his people (Col. 3:12; 1 Tim. 6:11).

Mercy; Merciful. Both these words occur in Matthew 5:7. *The merciful ones shall receive mercy.* The Greek words used most often translate a Hebrew word meaning kindness or lovingkindness. In his treatment of Matthew 5:7 William Barclay notes that the Hebrew word means the ability to get inside another's skin—to see through his eyes, feel with his feelings, and share in his sufferings. Without exception the noun is rendered "mercy" in all twenty-eight times it appears in the New Testament. Those who have obtained mercy should show the same (Matt. 18:21-35).

Messiah. The Hebrew word means "anointed," referring to the manner of consecrating kings and priests to their office by anointing with oil. In the New Testament the Greek form *Messias* is used (John 1:41; 4:25). The term is used of priests only with the adjective, "the anointed priest" (Lev. 3:5). The noun form is used to refer to kings, such as "the Lord's anointed" (2 Sam. 19:21). The pagan Cyrus is called "his anointed" or messiah since he was a chosen vessel to accomplish the Lord's will (Isa. 45:1). The term came to be used to refer to the anointed King of God's perfected kingdom (Dan. 9:25-26). By the time of Jesus the Jewish concept was that of a military-political Messiah. The Greek form is "Christ." It first was the title of an office, but came to be a personal name for the Savior (John 1:41; 1 Cor. 15:3). See *Jesus Christ*.

Michael. The name means "who is like God." It was a common one among the Israelites. The New Testament emphasis is upon Michael the archangel (Jude 9). He was regarded by the Jews as their guardian. Probably he is the archangel referred to in 1 Thessalonians 4:16. He also led the heavenly forces in repelling Satan's attack upon heaven (Rev. 12:7-9).

Middle Wall of Partition. This term is found in Ephesians 2:14 to refer to the division between Jews and Gentiles. The reference is to stone slabs in the Jerusalem Temple fastened to the wall at each entrance from the court of the Gentiles to the court of the women. No Gentile was permitted to go beyond this point (cf. Acts 21:28-29; 24:6).

A fragment of one stone and a complete one have been found. The latter is in a museum in Istanbul. It reads in Greek, "No man of another nation to enter within the balustrade and enclosure round the Temple, and whosoever is caught will have himself to blame that his death ensues." This meant that no Gentile had access to God in the Temple.

In Ephesians 2:14 Paul says that Christ has removed this barrier "for to make in himself of twain one new man, so making peace" (v. 15). In his atonement Christ has created a new order of mankind, the Christian, so that "through him we both [believing Gentiles and Jews] have access by one Spirit unto the Father" (v. 18). See *Reconciliation*.

Millennium. This is the Latin derivative which refers to the "thousand years" mentioned in Revelation 20:2-5,7. This figure has resulted in three schools of thought. *Postmillennial:* that after a thousand years of peace and prosperity on earth Christ will return. This position is not so popular now as it was in the early years of this century. *Premillennial:* that Christ will return before this period, and establish an earthly reign for a thousand years prior to his final return at the end of the age. This is a widely held position today. *Amillennial:* that the thousand years is a numerical symbol of a long but indefinite period of time extending from Jesus' ascension to his return (2 Pet. 3:3-13). This view is growing in popularity. In most circles one's position on eschatology is not a test of orthodoxy or fellowship. Able scholars are found holding to each view today, especially the second and third. Most Christian scholars hold to "the blessed hope, and the glorious appearing of the great God and our Saviour Jesus Christ" (Titus 2:13). See *Eschatology; Jesus Christ.*

Mind. This word renders two Greek words. One means "mind" (Rom. 1:28). The other is an intensive word which connotes more the idea of reflection or thinking through something to a greater depth of understanding (Heb. 8:10; 10:16). The latter word is used of loving God with all one's "mind" (Matt. 22:37; Mark 12:30; Luke 10:27). It is also used in the bad sense (Eph. 2:3; Col. 1:21). The former word also has the dual use: bad (1 Tim. 6:5); good (Rom. 12:2). The context must decide. This word is found in the Gospels only in Luke 24:45, "understanding."

Neither of these words is used purely of a mental process, but reaches down into the ethical sense. To the Greeks "mind" involved the entire inner man. See *Person; Personality.*

Miracle. The word "miracle" in the New Testament translates several words: one always rendered "wonder" meaning a portent (Matt. 24:24; Acts 2:22,43; 4:30); another stressing "power" (Matt. 22:29) or "mighty work" (Luke 10:13; 19:37); another meaning "sign" (John 2:18) or "miracle" (John 2:11; 10:41). Always in John's Gospel the word "miracle" means "sign"—signs of Jesus' deity. Miracles were evidences that God was in the new Christian movement.

Some see miracles as contrary to the laws of nature. But it should be added—as man understands them. Fifty years ago television would have been a *miracle.*

A miracle in the spiritual sense may be defined as an act of God, contrary to natural law as men understand it but not as God understands it, and done in accord with his will for the accomplishment of his benevolent, spiritual purpose.

Mystery. This word was used in pagan religions for secrets known only to the ones who practiced them. Certain religions were known as Mystery Religions. Cf. Eleusinian and Orphic Mysteries. Christianity also has its mysteries (Matt. 13:11; Mark 4:11; Luke 8:10). Out of twenty-seven uses in the New Testament twenty are found in Paul's writings. Evidently he used the word to cope with the Mystery Religions, saying that the Christian gospel also has its mysteries. To him a mystery was something hidden in the mind of God from eternity but revealed to man in Christ (Rom. 16:25-26; 1 Cor. 2:7; 15:51; Eph. 3:3-5). It was something to be received by revelation, not discovered through reason.

Paul's greatest mystery was God's purpose in Christ to save Gentiles as well as Jews (Eph. 3:6). This was social and spiritual dynamite in that day. The "fellowship of the mystery" is that this truth is to be made known through the church (Eph. 3:9-11).

Myth. See *Fable*.

Name. In both Testaments the word "name" may denote a person, place, or thing. But it is also used to denote a person's character or work (Matt. 1:21; 6:9). "Name" is used to refer to Jesus himself (Acts 5:41; 3 John 7). "For my name's sake" refers to the person of Christ (Matt. 10:22; 19:20). The "name" of Jesus connotes his authority (Mark 9:39; Acts 4:7). To believe in Christ's name is to believe in him (John 1:12; Acts 4:12). To preach in his name is to do so by his authority (Luke 24:47). To bow at his name is to do so before his person (Phil. 2:10). Christians are to pray in his name: by his authority and merit, in accord with his will, and in union with his person (John 14:13-14). See *Prayer*.

Needle. This English word appears only three times in the New Testament. Of interest is the fact that while Matthew 19:24 and Mark 10:25 use the word for a sewing needle, Luke 18:24 uses the one for a surgical needle. This reflects the fact that Luke was a physician. It shows also that the Holy Spirit inspired the message but left the writer free to choose his words.

Unsuccessful attempts have been made to relate this figure to a small gate in the wall of an ancient city. To pass through it a camel had to be unloaded and then go through on its knees. The idea expressed by Jesus is that one who trusts in riches rather than in him cannot enter the kingdom of God. See *Faith; Grace.*

Neighbor. This translates a word meaning "near," so a nigh-dweller. Jews sought to limit the command to love one's neighbor as himself (Lev. 19:18) to their own countrymen or Jews. In the parable of the Good Samaritan Jesus shows that a neighbor is anyone in need regardless of racial or other differences (Luke 10:25-37). He also placed the emphasis, not on defining a neighbor, but on being one (Luke 10:36-37). See *Love.*

New Birth. The term "new birth" refers to the spiritual experience of one who believes in Jesus Christ as Savior. The New Testament term is "born again" (John 3:3) or "born from above." The Greek word allows either sense. It is effected by the Holy Spirit (John 3:6). As one is born naturally with earthly relationships, so he must be born from above into heavenly or spiritual relationships. Only thus may one enter the kingdom and/or family of God. See *Adoption* and *Salvation.*

Noah, The Days of. Jesus' example of "the days of Noe" (Matt. 24:37-39) leads some to compare moral and spiritual conditions in Noah's day prior to the flood with present-day similarities as evidence of the imminent return of the Lord. But Jesus' point was that life in Noah's day went its normal way until suddenly the flood came. Life will proceed normally until suddenly, without warning Jesus will return. His coming is always imminent. See *Eschatology.*

Number. Numerical symbolism was widespread among the ancients. A number might be literal in value. But it often carries symbolic meaning, especially in apocalyptic writings like Revelation. Numbers such as 3,4,7,10, and 12 and their multiples are especially significant. For instance, 7 means perfection; 6 being less than 7 connotes imperfection. For a discussion of such numerology see "Number" in *The International Standard Bible Encyclopaedia,* Vol. IV, pages 2157-2163 and Ray Summers, *Worthy Is the Lamb* (Nashville: Broadman Press, 1951, pages 20-25). See *Beast, Mark of the.*

Nurture. The Greek word so translated in Ephesians 6:4 comes from the verb "to train a child." It is also rendered "chastening" (Heb. 12:5,7,11), "chastisement" (Heb. 12:8), and "instruction" (2 Tim. 3:16). The verb is used thirteen times with various renderings such as "chasten" (1 Cor. 11:32; Heb. 12:6-7,10), "chastise" (Luke 23:16,22), "teach" (Acts 22:3), "learn" (Acts 7:22; 1 Tim. 1:20), and "instruct" (2 Tim. 2:25).

Obedience; Obey. The Greek words so rendered mean to hear under. For instance, out of greater age and experience the parent speaks; from his lesser position the child hears under or obeys (Eph. 6:1; see 6:5). Even Jesus is said to have been "subject" to his parents. Though a different word is used (as troops under command), the idea is the same.

Christ is himself the perfect example of obedience. He was obedient to his Father's will in all things (John 4:34; see Luke 22:42). In his humanity he "learned obedience by the things which he suffered" (Heb. 5:8). He "became obedient unto death, even the death of the cross" (Phil. 2:8). This obedience was to his Father's redemptive will (see John 8:28-29; Heb. 10:9; see Rom. 5:19). Because of his absolute obedience, he was also "highly exalted" (Phil. 2:9). In Christ the Christian learns that he is not ready to excel until he learns to obey. See *Atonement.*

Omnipotence. This word is not found in the English Bible. But the adjective is found in Revelation 19:6. The Greek word so rendered is found as "Almighty" in 2 Corinthians 6:18; Revelation 1:8; 4:8; 11:17; 15:3; 16:7,14; 19:15; 21:22. The theological meaning of "omnipotence" is that God can do anything that is in keeping with his holy, righteous nature, purpose, and will. Luke 1:37 reads, literally, "Because not is impossible alongside God any word." What God says, he can do. See *God; Miracle.*

Omnipresence; Omniscience. Neither of these words appears in the Bible. But the ideas are there. The former means that God is present at all moments of time and in every part of space simultaneously (Psalm 139). He is in the universe but not contained by it. Because of his omnipresence God is omniscient. He possesses all knowledge simultaneously without the necessity of reason or thought (Job 34:21-22; Psalm 139:15-18; Isa. 29:15; Acts 1:24; 15:18; 1 John 1:5). Since he possesses all knowledge it follows that he knows events before they happen (note "foreknowledge, Acts 2:23). But foreknowledge of an event does not mean that one causes it. God knows who will receive or reject Jesus, but by his sovereign choice man is a free moral agent who acts in accord with his own will. See *Election.*

Only Begotten. These words render one Greek word used nine times in the New Testament. Other than in Luke 7:12; 8:42; 9:38; Hebrews 11:17 it refers to Christ as God's only begotten Son (John 1:14,18; 3:16,18; 1 John 4:9). Of Christ it means that he is God's unique Son. His uniqueness is evident in his deity, virgin birth, sinless life, atoning death, and his being the "firstfruits" of the resurrection from the dead (1 Cor. 15:20). He is God's Son essentially. Through faith in him men may become sons of God (John 1:12).

Jesus never referred to his relation to God in the same sense as that of believers' sonship. "I ascend unto my Father, and your Father; and to my God, and your God" (John 20:17). See *Virgin Birth.*

Ordinance. Basically this word means something commanded such as law, either governmental (Rom. 13:2; 1 Pet. 2:13), or religious (Heb. 9:1,10). In 1 Corinthians 11:2 it translates the word for something handed down from one generation to another or "traditions." While the word is not found in the New Testament for baptism and the Lord's Supper, they are so-called as their observance is commanded by the Lord.

Orphan. This is a transliteration of the Greek *orphanos,* meaning "fatherless" (James 1:27). To minister to such is one practice of pure, undefiled religion before God. Of special interest is its use by Jesus in John 14:18 where it is rendered "comfortless." When Jesus left the world his disciples were not left as orphans. He came to them in the person of the Holy Spirit. See *Holy Spirit.*

Palsy. This word translates the Greek word transliterated into English as "paralytic" (Matt. 4:24; 8:6; 9:2,6; Mark 2:3-5,9-10). It was one of many diseases healed by Jesus. See *Miracle.*

Panoply. This word meaning "all armor" is transliterated into English as the armor of a soldier (Luke 11:22; Eph. 6:11,13). When Paul dictated Ephesians he was chained to a Roman soldier. In Ephesians 6:14-17 he gives a spiritual application to a Roman soldier's entire armor except the spear used and greaves or shin guards worn in battle. A soldier on guard duty such as this would not need a spear or greaves. Note that the only offensive weapon of the Christian is "the sword of the Spirit, which is the word of God" (v. 17; cf. Rev. 19:15,21). One can destroy spiritual enemies (Eph. 6:12) only with spiritual weapons. The armor listed by Paul protects only the front. No Roman or Christian soldier should turn his back to the enemy.

Parable. This comes from the Greek verb meaning "to cast alongside." Jesus often taught by parables as he cast a spiritual truth alongside an earthly reality (see Matt. 13:1-52; Mark 4:1-34; Luke 8:4-17). In the New Testament only Jesus taught with parables. They were intended to reveal truth to Jesus' friends but to conceal it from his enemies who would only use his teachings against him.

Someone has described a parable as an earthly story with a heavenly meaning. Or as a handle by which to take hold of spiritual truth, like illustrations in a sermon.

Paraclete. See *Holy Spirit.*

Paradise. This transliterates a Greek word derived from the Hebrew. It probably was of Persian origin, meaning a royal park or fenced-in garden. Jesus used the word only once (Luke 23:43). But see 2 Corinthians 12:4; Revelation 2:7, the only other uses in the New Testament. Some would distinguish between Paradise and Heaven. But these references seem to mean Heaven itself (see Rev. 22). See *Heaven.*

Parousia. While this word as such does not appear in the King James Version, in its Greek form it is used twenty-four times in the New Testament. Except for 2 Corinthians 10:10 and Philippians 2:12 where it is rendered "presence," it otherwise reads "coming" (cf. Matt. 24:3,27,37,39; 1 Cor. 15:23; 16:17; 2 Cor. 7:6-7; Phil. 1:26; 1 Thess. 2:19; 3:13; 4:15; 5:23; 2 Thess. 2:1,8,9; James 5:7-8; 2 Pet. 1:16; 3:4,12; 1 John 2:28). From these uses it is evident that its principal use is with reference to the Lord's return. The Greek word means "being alongside." It was used of a ruler visiting parts of his realm. In this sense it is meaningful as to the Lord's return.

Passion. This word comes from the Latin *passio* which is related to a Greek word which basically means to suffer. In the King James Version "passion" in the singular appears only one time where it refers to the redemptive suffering of Christ (Acts 1:3). A kindred word is so rendered "suffer" in Acts 26:23. In Colossians 1:24 another like word refers to Jesus' suffering prior to the cross. This word is also used of man's suffering for Christ (Rom. 8:18; 2 Cor. 1:5-7). "Of like passions" (Acts 14:15; James 5:17) renders a compound form of a word of this family meaning "of like nature" or "emotions."

One word of this family *(pathos)* is used respectively in Romans 1:26; Colossians 3:5; 1 Thessalonians 4:5 as evil *affection, inordinate affection,* and *lust.*

Pastor. See *Elder.*

Patience. In the New Testament this word twice translates a Greek word which means "longsuffering" (Heb. 6:12; James 5:10). The usual word rendered "patience" (thirty-two times) means an abiding under (cf. Rom. 5:3-4; Col. 1:11; 1 Thess. 1:3; Rev. 2:2-3,19; 13:10b; 14:12).

In English this word connotes passive endurance. But in non-biblical literature the Greek word expressed the quality of an athlete or soldier to take all his opponent could throw against him and still have reserve strength to counterassault to victory. The word has been found in the sense of a military citation, "a patient soldier." This sense greatly enhances the idea in the Christian virtue of patience.

Paul; Saul. On his first missionary journey "Saul" suddenly becomes "Paul" (Acts 13:9,13). The most likely explanation is that he had two names: Saul (Jewish); Paul (Roman). When he and Barnabas entered pagan Gentile territory he began using the Roman name.

Peace. The Greek word rendered "peace" (*eirēnē*, note "Irene") has much the same sense as the Hebrew *Shālōm.* They connote freedom from disturbance, outward and inward; soundness; prosperity; well-being in general, especially in relation to both God and man (Eph. 2:13-19). Both were used as greetings (John 20:19,21; 1 Cor. 1:3). Christians are to live in peace with one another (Mark 9:50; 2 Cor. 13:11). God is the Author and Giver of peace (Rom. 15:33).This is a peace beyond human comprehension (Phil. 4:7). Christians are to be peacemakers, in which role they will be recognized as sons of God (Matt. 5:9). The peace of God is to "rule" or serve as an umpire in all Christian relationships (Col. 3:15).

Peace in the Christian sense is not governed by outward circumstances. It is an inner calm which abides in a storm (John 14:27; 16:32-33).

Pentecost. The feast of Pentecost was second only to Tabernacles as great Jewish harvest festivals. They celebrated the former and latter harvests respectively, much like Thanksgiving. Pentecost came fifty days after Passover. Its Christian significance lies in the fact that on this day the Holy Spirit came upon the church in power to begin his ministry in propagating the gospel (Acts 2:1ff.). This event changed the disciples from a frightened, despairing group into an invincible army.

The phenomena at Pentecost were *sound, sight, speech,* and *power:* a sound not of wind but "as of a rushing mighty wind"; a sight not of fire but "cloven tongues as of fire"; the ability of the disciples to speak languages other than their own without previous study; and the power of the Holy Spirit. The first three were temporary; the fourth remains. See *Holy Spirit* and *Tongues, Speaking in.*

Perdition. This word renders a Greek word which means "ruin" or "loss" (John 17:12; Phil. 1:28; 2 Thess. 2:3; 1 Tim. 6:9; Heb. 10:39; 2 Pet. 3:7; Rev. 17:8,11). It is also used as "destruction" (Matt. 7:13; 9:22) and "waste" (Matt. 26:8; Mark 14:4 which may apply to Heb. 10:39).

In the spiritual sense it is the opposite of salvation. A "lost" person is one separated from God by sin. Jesus came to seek and to save, bring back to God, that which was lost (Matt. 18:11). To be spiritually lost is spiritual death (Eph. 2:1). In the final spiritual sense "perdition" is the equivalent of hell (Rev. 17:8,11).

The "son of Perdition" is applied to Judas Iscariot (John 17:12) and the Antichrist (2 Thess. 2:3). This refers to both character and destiny. See *Gehenna; Hell.*

Perfect. In the New Testament this word translates one which expresses the idea of completeness or having reached a goal. It may mean to fulfil the purpose of one's being. Thus God is complete in all his being, and Christians should strive to be the same (Matt. 5:48; cf. 19:21). In Ephesians 4:13 "perfect" may read adult or mature.

Perfect does not necessarily mean free from fault or aim. Such a condition is never promised to the Christian in this life. But perfection in God does mean completeness, fulfiling the purpose of his being, and freedom from imperfection—moral and otherwise. The Christian should ever strive for this goal because it is there. And in Christ he has the power to progress toward the goal (Heb. 13:21). Unattainable in this life? Yes. But ever a challenge to walk in the steps of the Savior. See *Salvation.*

Perseverance. See *Security of the Believer.*

Person; Personality. One time in the New Testament "person" translates a word meaning "that which lies under" (Heb. 1:3). It means the very substance of something or someone, as "the very image of his substance" or "person."

Otherwise, "person" renders a word meaning "before the eyes" or "before the face" (Matt. 22:16; Gal. 2:6). This word is translated "face" fifty-five times and "person" seven times (Matt. 22:16; Mark 12:14; Luke 20:21; 2 Cor. 1:11; 2:10; Gal. 2:6; Jude 16); it is rendered "countenance" three times (Luke 9:29; Acts 2:28; 2 Cor. 3:7b).

Combinations of this word with one meaning "receiving" is rendered "respect of person" (Acts 10:34; Rom. 2:11; Eph. 6:9; Col. 3:25; James 2:1,9). They mean that one should not or God does not receive a man on the basis of his face. In each case the context relates it to man or God. Note that racial features are found in the face.

"Personality" is that indefinable quality which characterizes a person. *Per-sona* is the Latin word "person." It comes from the idea of an actor speaking through a mask which denoted the role he played. *Sona* came to be identified with the actor; and finally, to the character of an individual. As used of men it distinguishes them from mere animals. It involves the fact that man is made in God's image (Gen. 1:27). He is a finite person, a being of choice and self-determination—thus responsible for his choices. God is the supreme Personality (Rom. 11:34,36). The human personality is spiritual, and, therefore, survives bodily death. In Christ he becomes again clothed with a spiritual or Spirit-controlled body (Phil. 3:21; 1 Cor. 15:44). Man is a human personality; Christ is a divine Personality. See *Immortality; Life.*

Pharisees; Sadducees. There were two prominent religious-political parties among the Jews in Jesus' time. They were at opposite ends of the poles in both areas of life. The origin of both sects is shrouded in mystery. Though some would trace the Sadducees from a more ancient origin, both probably arose during the period following the Babylonian captivity.

The "Pharisees" were the "separatists," derived from the Hebrew *parash*, to separate. They probably emerged as the group which strongly opposed efforts to force Greek culture and religion on the Jews during the period between the Old and New Testaments. At that time they rendered a great service to Judaism. But by the time of Jesus they largely had degenerated into a dry ceremonial, legalistic group.

They were the *strict party* in Judaism: held all the Old Testament as genuine Scripture, believed in angels, miracles, and the resurrection of the dead with a final judgment of rewards and punishments. They had a strong messianic hope, and were violently opposed to Roman rule over the Jews. More numerous than the Sadducees, they exercised less political power. Though as a group they opposed Jesus, there were some who did not (cf. Nicodemus, John 3:1, and probably Joseph of Arimathea, Mark 15:43). Both were members of the Sanhedrin. Saul of Tarsus (Paul) was a Pharisee (Phil. 3:5). However, as a group they received Jesus' most excoriating denunciation (Matt. 23).

The Sadducees derived their name from some Zadok. During this period all the high priests were of this party. Thus they exercised greater power in religion, since the high priest was head of the

Sanhedrin. In theology they accepted only the five books of Moses (Pentateuch) as Scripture; denied miracles, angels, and the resurrection of the dead. Since under the Romans they enjoyed considerable political power and wealth they were for the *status quo*. As such they were more concerned about their *place* than their *nation* (note the order in John 11:48).

Though archenemies of the Pharisees, they finally joined forces with them in opposition to Jesus (Matt. 16:1; John 11:47-53). The Pharisees opposed Jesus largely with words, but as realists it was the Sadducees which took the lead in his death. When he restored Lazarus to life right under their noses in nearby Bethany, the Sadducees vowed to bring him to his death (John 11:49-53). But the Pharisees were willing accomplices. Their common cause against Jesus led to a temporary truce. But their basic differences remained (Acts 23:1-10).

Philosophy. This word appears only in Colossians 2:8 in a warning against philosophy (love of wisdom) characterized by empty deceit. Paul did not oppose philosophy as such, but a particular one which degraded Christ (Gnosticism, which see). In essence, he said one should judge his philosophy by Christ, not Christ by his philosophy.

Phylactery. This word is found in the New Testament only in Matthew 23:5. It refers to a little box worn on either the arm or forehead, and containing certain Scriptures (cf. Exod. 13:11-16; Deut. 6:4-5; 11:13-16[?]). Note the word "frontlets" (Exod. 11:16; Deut. 6:8; 11:18). What God had spoken figuratively as a reminder of his word, the Pharisees took literally. They even thought that the larger the phylactery the greater their piety. So they became symbolic of hypocrisy. See *Hypocrisy*.

Prayer. This word translates a number of Greek words ranging all the way from asking a favor to loving communion with God. Someone defined prayer as a wish or desire turned heavenward. In this sense prayer comes from a sense of need and faith that God will supply that need in accord with his benevolent will and purpose (Heb. 11:6). The Christian view of prayer springs from the prayer life of Jesus (Mark 1:35; 14:32-39). Luke places a great emphasis upon his prayer life (3:21; 6:12; 9:16,29; 22:32,39-46; 23:34,46). What is commonly called the "Lord's Prayer" is really the "Model Prayer" (Matt. 6:9-13). John 17 is Jesus' *High Priestly* prayer. If Jesus needed to pray, how much greater is that need for his followers! Prayer is to be offered to the Father in the name of the Son (John 16:23-24,26). Such should be offered by Jesus' authority and merit, and in accord with the Father's will (John 15:7).

Paul both practiced prayer (Eph. 3:14-19) and urged his readers to pray (Rom. 12:12; Phil. 4:6). To "pray without ceasing" (1 Thess. 5:17) means to live in the custom and attitude of prayer. One's prayer life is enhanced by the Holy Spirit (Jude 20; cf. Rom. 8:26-27). As one has said, in the New Testament sense prayer is offered to the Father, in the name of Christ as Mediator, and through the enabling grace of the Holy Spirit. See *Mediator; Mediation.*

Preach. This word renders two Greek words: one meaning to declare good news (gospel) or *evangelize* (Acts 5:42); the other to herald the gospel (Matt. 3:1). The use of these words is almost evenly divided in the New Testament (former, fifty-five times; latter, sixty-one times). Of special interest is the fact that the latter was used of a king's herald proclaiming his message throughout his realm; he was to be obeyed as if the king personally did it (cf. 2 Cor. 4:5). This verb was also used of one who announced the participants in an athletic contest. This has bearing on 1 Corinthians 9:27. Paul did not want to announce those in the contest and then lose it himself. He wanted to be a winner in all he did for Christ.

Predestination. Unfortunately this word is colored by theological presuppositions rather than the meaning in the Greek words so translated. This word does not mean fatalism—that only some are predestined for salvation with all others excepted.

The word rendered "predestinate" (Rom. 8:29-30; Eph. 1:5,11) means to set a boundary beforehand. The basic verb means "to horizon" *(horizō)* with the prefix meaning "beforehand." In Ephesians 1 the boundary is "in Christ" (see *Election*). God has chosen or elected that those who are in Christ will be saved. Others *outside Christ* will be lost. Predestination never violates man's free will.

Two other words related to this doctrine mean "foreknowledge (Acts 2:23; Rom. 8:29; 11:2; 1 Pet. 1:2) and "purpose," that which is placed before (Eph. 3:11). God's purpose is to save all who believe in Christ. His foreknowledge of an event does not necessarily mean that he caused it. The context must decide.

Preeminence. This word means to have the first place. In Colossians 1:18 it means that Christ has the first place in both the natural and spiritual universe. Third John 9 renders a compound word to *love the first place* among men. The former is good; the latter is bad.

Prevent. This word appears twice in the New Testament (Matt. 17:25; 1 Thess. 4:15). In old English it meant to come before. The Greek words so translated carry the same idea. In Matthew the basic word is prefixed with *pro,* before. Jesus spoke probably in anticipation of Peter's question. The primary doctrinal interest lies in the word "prevent" in 1 Thessalonians. Here it means that those believers alive at the Lord's return will not leave behind those Christians who die prior to that event. They will first be resurrected. The living will be transformed in body (1 Cor. 15:50-57), and the two groups together shall be caught up to meet the Lord in the air. See *Resurrection.*

Principalities. This word renders the Greek word for "head" or "beginning" (John 1:1). In Titus 3:1 it is used in the plural for earthly rulers. Elsewhere in the plural it refers to superhuman agencies either angelic or demonic (Rom. 8:38; Eph. 1:21; 3:10; 6:12; Col. 1:16; 2:10,15). In each case the context makes clear the exact sense.

Proselyte; God-fearer. "Proselyte" comes from a Greek word meaning "I come to" or "approach." It was used four times in the New Testament (Matt. 23:15; Acts 2:10; 6:5; 13:43). A proselyte was a Gentile who had become a Jew in religion by circumcision, baptism, making certain sacrifices, and living by the Mosaic law and the many rules of conduct contained in current Judaism.

A God-fearer was a Gentile who was studying Judaism with the possibility of becoming a proselyte. But he had not yet done so. Cornelius was a "God-fearer" or one that "feared God" (Acts 10:2,22; cf. Acts 13:16,26).

Punishment, Everlasting. Everlasting punishment assumes the survival of the soul after death (Matt. 10:28; Luke 16:19-31). Also that sin results in retribution (Isa. 3:10-11; Matt. 11:22-24; Rom. 2:5-11). The question is as to whether it is everlasting, temporary, or does it result in annihilation? The New Testament does not imply any second chance for repentance and salvation after death. First Peter 3:19-20 most likely means that through the Spirit the Lord preached to "the spirits [now] in prison" during Noah's day. Revelation 22:11a clearly speaks against this idea of a second chance. Those holding to soul annihilation find this idea in such words as "destruction" and "perishing." However, such do not mean a cessation of existence, but a disordering of being in eternal separation from God, the intended home of the soul.

"Everlasting" renders a word meaning "age." It is used in John 3:16 of "age-abiding life." In Matthew 25:46 "everlasting" (punishment) and "eternal" (life) render the same Greek word. If there is no everlasting punishment, there is no everlasting life. But the New Testament teaches both. On everlasting punishment see *Hell; Gehenna; Retribution.*

Python. This word appears only once in the Bible (Acts 16:16) where it is rendered "a spirit of divination" ("a spirit, a Python"). This word was associated with the Oracle at Delphi. It probably means here some form of ventriloquism.

Quick; Quicken. The word so translated came from a Greek verb meaning to give life or make alive. As used in the New Testament it relates to the resurrection from the dead (1 Cor. 15:36; Eph. 2:5; Col. 2:13; cf. John 5:21).

Quiet. The words rendered "to be quiet" (1 Thess. 4:11) mean "to refrain from gossip or meddlesomeness." But the derived meaning is also gentleness and a life free from trouble (1 Pet. 3:4; see 1 Tim. 2:2). In Acts 24:2 "quietness" renders the word for "peace." See *Peace.*

Quit. The only time this word appears in the New Testament it translates a verb meaning "to behave like a man" (1 Cor. 16:13).

Rabbi. Used by Jews as a title of respect for teachers, its root Hebrew meaning is "great," so "my great one." It is used seventeen times in the New Testament. It is used of Christ fourteen times

("Master" or Teacher, Matt. 26:25,49; Mark 9:5; 11:21; 14:45; John 4:31; 9:2; 11:8; "Rabbi," John 1:38,49; 3:2,26; 6:25). It is rendered "rabbi" in Matthew 23:7-8. *Rabboni* is a Galilean form of this word (Mark 10:51, "Lord"; John 20:16). See *Judas Iscariot.*

Raca; Fool. "Raca" is an Aramaic word meaning "empty." It was a term of contempt used by the Jews in Jesus' day, and appears only once in the New Testament (Matt. 5:22). In this verse Jesus shows that murder is rooted in the attitude of the heart. Note the growing attitudes and punishments: "anger" ("without a cause" not in best texts), punishable by provincial courts; "Raca," punishable by the "council" or Sanhedrin; "fool," *in danger* of "hell fire" or Gehenna (see *Hell*). *Raca* refers to one's intellectual ability ("you simpleton"); "fool" refers to one's character or moral and spiritual life ("you rascal"). Jesus warns against degrading human personality and value which could evolve into the overt act of murder. See *Person; Personality.*

Ransom; Redemption. These are kindred words in English as well as in Greek. But in Greek the words come from a common root verb, "to loose" or "set free." Thus the word for "ransom" (Matt. 20:28) means that which secures freedom such as paying the price to free a slave. From kindred words come "redemption" (Heb. 9:12) and "redeemer" (Acts 7:35, "deliverer"). The word most often used for "redemption" is a compound word "a redemption from" which best reads "full redemption" (Luke 21:28; Rom. 3:24; 8:23; 1 Cor. 1:30; Eph. 1:7,14; 4:30; Col. 1:14; Heb. 9:15; 11:35, "deliverance").

In redemption the ransom is the atoning death of Christ (Rom. 6:23). This ransom was not paid to Satan to gain release of those held in his slavery, else he would be greater than God. The ransom was paid in order that God may forgive the sins of the believer in Jesus Christ (Rom. 3:23-26). See *Atonement* and *Reconcile; Reconciliation.*

Reconcile; Reconciliation. The basic idea in these words is "to exchange." Since God does not need to be reconciled to man, the idea is for man to exchange his sinful, rebellious way for that of God: to receive God's righteousness through faith in Christ, and to do God's will in his life. This change is elsewhere expressed by repentance (which see). The basic Greek verb is used only six times (Rom. 5:10; 1 Cor. 7:11; 2 Cor. 5:18-20), with the noun form used four times (Rom. 5:11, "atonement"; 11:15, "reconciling"; 2 Cor. 5:18-19). A compound form of the verb is used three times (Eph. 2:16; Col. 1:20-21), which emphasizes the idea of reconciliation. With respect to human relations see Matthew 5:24 (to be changed throughout) and 1 Corinthians 7:11. Hebrews 2:17 renders a different verb meaning "to appease" or "to propitiate" (see 1 John 2:2; 4:10). It is related to the idea of mercy (Luke 18:13, same verb).

Second Corinthians 5:18-21 is perhaps the most important passage on this theme. It shows that God was in Christ effecting reconciliation (v. 19) and how it was done (v. 21). Also it shows the place of the Christian in bringing this work to bear upon a lost world (vv. 19b-20). God pleads through them as they plead in the place of Christ. When the Christian pleads with a lost person it should be regarded as God in Christ doing the pleading. To refuse the Christian's message is to refuse God in Christ. See *Preach.*

Regeneration. See *New Birth; Salvation.*

Remission of Sins. The two Greek words rendered "remission" mean respectively "to let go" or "send away" and "leave undone" or "let fall alongside." Both are used in the sense of forgiving debts and/or wrongs. The noun form of the latter is used in the New Testament only in Romans 3:25 where it may read a *passing over* without punishment. The noun of the former is rendered "remission" nine times (Matt. 26:28; Mark 1:4; Luke 1:77; 3:3; 24:47; Acts 2:38; 10:43; Heb. 9:22; 10:18), and "forgiveness" six times (Mark 3:29; Acts 5:31; 13:38; 26:18; Eph. 1:7; Col. 1:14).

In the spiritual sense "remission" means forgiveness of sin as a debt against God. It does not mean that he is indifferent to sin, but that in Christ he has created the condition whereby he may graciously forgive all who believe in his Son as Savior.

Repent; Repentance. Two Greek verbs are translated "repent" in the New Testament. One is used six times (Matt. 21:29,32; 27:3; 2 Cor. 7:8; Heb. 7:21). It means a change of feelings as to past actions but more in the sense of regret. It may or may not result in true repentance. Judas regretted his betrayal of Jesus but had no change of heart; thus he hanged himself.

The verb for true repentance means a change of mind, heart, and attitude. It is used thirty-four times in the New Testament; the noun form appears twenty-four times. Another word meaning a complete turning about (Acts 9:35; 1 Thess. 1:9) also expresses this idea. Wherever "repent" or "repentance" is used other than the cited references for the former verb the meaning is a complete change in life's direction or true repentance. Unfortunately the English word "repent" is of Latin derivation, and carries the idea of *penance*. But true repentance calls for a complete change in attitude, conduct, mind, and will with respect to God, sin, and Satan. See *Faith*.

Rest. The English word "pause" is from the Latin *pausa* which is from the Greek *pausis* which basically means a temporary stop or rest. From this basic Greek verb come compound verbs (combined with a preposition) to express various ideas of rest. One such verb means "to rest again" or "to refresh" (Matt. 11:28; 26:45; see also 1 Cor. 16:18; 2 Cor. 7:13, "refresh"). Another such word means "to rest down" or thoroughly (Heb. 4:4,8,10). The noun form is found in Acts 7:49; Hebrews 3:11,18; 4:1,3,5,10,11. The references in Hebrews compare this to the *rest* of Israel in Canaan after her wilderness wanderings. Some see this as heaven.

However, in Hebrews 4:9 "rest" renders *sabbatismos,* a Sabbath-kind of rest. This word apparently appears nowhere else in Greek literature (a doubtful use in Plutarch). It seems, therefore, that the author coined this word to refer to a particular kind of rest. "Sabbath" means "rest." God rested from his creative work, but continued his providential and redemptive work—not a complete cessation of activity as seen in the other word for "rest" in Hebrews 4. The writer sees these uses of "rest" as, in Israel's case in achieving Canaan, the Christian's development into a fit servant of God to be used in proclaiming his redemptive work. "Rest" in Hebrews 4:9 connotes, like God's continued work in redemption, the Christian's work in fulfilling his place in God's redemptive plan. (See Herschel H. Hobbs, *How to Follow Jesus* [Nashville: Broadman, 1971], pages 41-49.)

Resurrection. The basic Greek word means a "standing again" or up. The word "raise" is also used in this sense (cf. Acts 3:15; Rom. 4:24). This word is also used of the raising of Lazarus (John 12:1,9,17). The difference between these words is seen in this light. Lazarus was not resurrected to die no more. His was a resuscitation Of course, when "raise" is used of Jesus it means "resurrection." The noun rendered "resurrection" ("rising again," Luke 2:34) is used forty-two times (cf. Matt. 22:23; Acts 1:22; 1 Cor. 15:12). The very word denies that only the spirit lives on after death; the spirit does not die. So "resurrection" refers to a bodily resurrection (1 Cor. 15; see Luke 24:3,36-43; John 20:19-28).

Both the lost and saved will be raised (John 5:29; 2 Cor. 5:10; 2 Tim. 4:1). Some see two resurrections, one of the saved and another of the lost (see Rev. 20:5-6). In the light of John 5:29 the writer sees the "first" resurrection as referring to the regeneration experience (see Eph. 3:5-6). Jesus called himself "the resurrection, and the life" (John 11:25). His resurrection is the guarantee of that of his people (1 Cor. 15:20,23). See *Jesus Christ*.

Resurrection, Proof of Christ's. Among proofs to doubters of Jesus' bodily resurrection are the following. (1) The empty tomb. (2) The change in the disciples. (3) The witness of Paul (cf. 1 Cor. 15). (4) The Gospels' record. (5) The church through the ages. (6) Personal experience with Christ.

The Gospels are reliable records. All agree that Jesus' body was placed in the tomb on Friday and that it was empty on Sunday. All save Mark list appearances of the risen Lord (The best texts of Mark end with 16:8). Psychologically only such could transform the disciples from frightened rabbits to brave lions. By the same token the church could not be built upon fraud. Paul, among other things, cites above five hundred who saw Jesus alive at one time (no hallucination), most of whom lived when he wrote and could verify the fact (1 Cor. 15:6). One may debate another's logic but not his personal experience.

Retribution. This word is not used in the Bible. But the idea is found throughout. It is expressed as God's law in operation (Gal. 6:7-8). It is contained in such words as "punishment" (Matt. 25:46), "vengeance" (Rom. 12:19), and "wrath" (Matt. 3:7,12; John 3:36; Rom. 1:18; 2:3-5; 4:15; Eph. 5:6; Col. 3:6; 1 Thess. 1:10). Judgment implies retribution (Matt. 16; 27; 25:31-46). The very moral and righteous nature of God calls for retribution upon those who violate it. Or else the entire universe is nonmoral.

Revelation, Inspiration, Illumination. The very nature of God implies revelation. For God is love; and love reveals itself (1 John 4:8). The religion of the Bible is supernatural; it is received by divine revelation, not discovered through human reason.

"Revelation" translates a Greek word meaning "unveiling." God has revealed himself through nature (Rom. 1:19-20; cf. Psalm 8:3; 19:1-2), in the human conscience (Rom. 2:14-15, see *Conscience*), through the prophets (Heb. 1:1), and through the Bible (Rom. 2:17-18; cf. Luke 24:27,44-45). God's supreme revelation is in his Son (Heb. 1:2; cf. Matt. 1:23; John 1:1,14,18; 10:30; 14:9).

"Inspiration" means to breathe in. It refers to God's act through the Holy Spirit whereby he enabled chosen men to receive and record his revelation (2 Pet. 1:21). Second Timothy 3:16 reads, "All scripture is given by inspiration of God" or "God-breathed." Some see the Holy Spirit as giving the writers the exact words to use. Others see the Spirit as inspiring men, but leaving them free to choose their words. Since in parallel accounts on occasion the Gospel writers use different words (see *Kingdom of God* and *Needle*), the latter position seems to the writer to be the correct view. But both groups see the Spirit guarding the writers from error. The main thing is not the *method* but the *product*. And that is that the Bible is the Word of God, truth without any mixture of error for its substance. This, of course, refers to the original manuscripts. The Holy Spirit no more protects copyists than typesetters from error.

"Illumination" refers to the Spirit's work in enlightening men's minds and hearts that they may understand the Scriptures (John 14:26; 16:3). See *Bible; Holy Spirit; Jesus Christ*.

Reward. This word is of particular interest as used in Matthew 6:2,5,16; "They have their reward" renders one Greek word meaning "They are paid in full." If men give alms, pray, and fast to be seen of men, men see them; but God does not. They get what they seek. *Paid in full!*

Righteousness. This word belongs to a family of words which mean "just," "justify" (declare righteous), and "righteousness." In the New Testament "righteous" may refer to one who lived by the Mosaic law and looked down upon those who did not (Matt. 1:19, "just"; Rom. 5:7). "Justify" when used of God means his judicial act in declaring one righteous or in a state of justification (Rom. 8:30). This, of course, is not done arbitrarily but on the basis of one's faith in Christ and his saving work.

"Righteousness" refers to what God is in his nature (Rom. 10:3a), what he demands in man but which man cannot achieve within himself (Rom. 10:3b), and, therefore, which God provides in Christ (Rom. 10:3c-13). It is in this last sense that "righteousness" is expressed in the gospel (Rom. 1:17). It is the God-kind of righteousness. In this sense the word refers not to an attribute but an activity of God, whereby in Christ he picks one up out of the wrong and places him down in the right as though he had not been in the wrong.

Redeemed man is not righteous within himself; he possesses by grace through faith the righteousness of God which is in Christ Jesus (cf. Rom. 3:26). It is "from faith to faith," a matter of faith from beginning to end. Of course, such a person should show by his works that he is a child of God (Eph. 2:10; James 2:14-26). See *Atonement; Grace.*

Sabbath. See *Lord's Day.*

Sacrifice. The practice of animal sacrifice dates from the earliest beginnings of man (Gen. 4:4-5; 8:20-21; 13:4; 15:9-10). In the Old Testament this practice reached its zenith in the Mosaic code.

The New Testament presents Christ as the fulfilment of this system (cf. John 1:29; Acts 8:32-35; Rom. 5:8-10; 1 Cor. 1:17-18; Phil. 2:8). The author of Hebrews declares that Christ, in his once-for-all sacrifice, fulfilled the Old Testament system of repeated sacrifices (9:1 to 10:18).

Sadducees. See *Pharisees.*

Saints. This word renders a Greek word meaning "holy ones" or "set apart ones" (1 Cor. 1:2; 2 Cor. 1:1). All Christians are saints though they may not always act saintly (see the Corinthian epistles; Rom. 16:2; Eph. 5:3). Unfortunately the historical use of the word has all but blotted out the New Testament sense. Of course, New Testament saints should endeavor to live according to the holiness of God. See *Salvation*.

Salt. Jesus used this word figuratively (Matt. 5:13). Salt preserved, healed, and gave zest. Christians should be these things in the world. Colossians 4:6 probably means that one's speech should not be insipid.

Salvation. The Greek verb "to save" and its derivatives cover a wide range of meanings: to heal (Matt. 9:22), to save from danger (Matt. 8:25; Acts 27:20), to solve a problem (Phil. 2:12), to be saved spiritually (Rom. 1:16). The context must decide in each case (cf. Matt. 14:30; 27:42,49; John 12:27). In this brief sketch the concern is spiritual salvation.

Of course, for one to be saved he must be convicted of sin (John 16:8-11), experience repentance from sin (Luke 13:1-5), and have faith in Jesus Christ as Savior (John 5:24; Acts 16:30-31). This experience involves the atonement wrought by God in Christ and made effective in one's life by grace through faith through his Holy Spirit.

"Salvation" is used in the New Testament as regeneration (John 3:3), sanctification (Heb. 2:3), and glorification (Heb. 9:28). This threefold experience is expressed by the Greek word rendered "full redemption" (cf. Eph. 1:7,14; Col. 1:14; Heb. 9:15). *Regeneration* or the new birth is an instantaneous experience. Simultaneously the believer is *sanctified* by the indwelling of the Holy Spirit (John 14:17; Rom. 8:9; 1 Cor. 6:19) or set apart as a vessel dedicated to the service of God (cf. John 17:19). He is a "saint" (1 Cor. 1:2) or "holy one." The Christian does not grow into sanctification but should grow in it. *Glorification* is the sum total of glory and reward of the Christian in heaven, including the resurrection of the body (Rom. 8:17,23,29-30).

Regeneration is the salvation of the soul; sanctification is the saving of the Christian life; glorification is the heavenly state. In regeneration one is saved from the *penalty* of sin; in sanctification one is saved from the *power* of sin; in glorification one is saved from the *presence* of sin. In this threefold sense it is proper to say, "I am saved; I am being saved; I will be saved." See *Adoption*.

Sanhedrin. This word is composed of two Greek words meaning "seated together." Made up of seventy-one members, including the high priest as its chief officer, it probably was patterned after the seventy elders of Israel plus Moses (Num. 11:16). In Jesus' day this body ruled under the Romans in civil and religious matters. But Rome itself handled capital cases (Matt. 27:1-2). It was abolished after the destruction of the Jewish nation in 70 A.D. See *Trial of Jesus.*

Satan; Devil. Satan is a created but personal, superhuman, evil being, the adversary of both God and man, and second only to the triune God in power. "Satan" means "adversary." He is also called "devil," "accuser" or "slanderer." In Eden he slandered God to man (Gen. 3:1-5). In Job 1-2 he slandered man to God. Among other names given him are the following: Beelzebub (Matt. 12:24); enemy (Matt. 13:39); wicked one (Matt. 13:38); deceiver (Rev. 12:9); dragon (Rev. 12:3); father of lies and murderer (John 8:44); roaring lion (1 Pet. 5:8); Apollyon or destroyer (Rev. 9:11).

Satan makes a false claim to sovereignty in the world (Luke 4:6). Christ was manifested to prove this claim false (cf. Matt. 28:18; 1 John 3:8; Rev. 11:15). But Jesus called Satan the "prince of this world," predicting his ultimate defeat (John 12:31). While powerful, God puts a limit upon Satan's power and work (Job 1:12; 2:6). Satan's final end is to be cast into the lake of fire (Rev. 20:10).

Of interest is the fact that in the Bible Satan never appears to man as Satan (Gen. 3:1; 2 Cor. 11:14). But before God he always appears as Satan (Job 1-2; Matt. 4:1-11). God knows him for who he is. See *Demons; Temptation.*

Savior. See *Atonement; Jesus Christ.*

Schoolmaster. This term appears only in Galatians 3:24-25, where it renders a Greek word meaning "child-leader." Such a person was not a teacher but a slave charged with looking after a child. He was to see to his conduct, companions, safety, and to develop the child morally. When the child was old enough to go to school, this person gave him safe conduct, and then turned him over to the teacher. Paul likens the Mosaic law to this person whose purpose ultimately was to bring his charge to Christ the Teacher.

Security of the Believer. This simply means that when one truly believes in Jesus as Savior he is *saved* and *safe*. He is saved by God's grace and kept by God's grace (Eph. 2:8-10). Literally, "For by grace have ye been saved," a finished, permanent work. The New Testament abounds in similar promises (cf. John 3:16, "everlasting" is everlasting; 5:24; 10:27-29; 2 Cor. 1:22; Col. 3:3; 2 Tim. 1:12).

Ephesians 1:13-14 says that the Holy Spirit indwelling the Christian's body (John 14:17; 1 Cor. 6:19) is God's seal of ownership, and his "earnest" or guarantee to save unto *full-redemption* (see *Redemption* and *Salvation*) those who are his. The word rendered "earnest" means *earnest money*. It is found in the papyri in this sense. Also it is used only three times in the New Testament and always in connection with the Holy Spirit (2 Cor. 1:22; 5:5; Eph. 1:14). One puts up earnest money to guarantee that he will complete a transaction. If he fails, he loses his earnest money. In his Holy Spirit God has pledged his very being that he will save and keep safe all who believe in his Son. So long as God is, so long is the Christian safe. One can ask for no greater guarantee.

Space does not permit a full treatment of passages cited to the contrary. But note Galatians 5:4. This epistle was written to refute the idea that one is saved by works plus faith in Jesus. The picture here is two ways men choose in search after salvation: the law way and the grace way. One cannot travel both ways. For works cancel out grace. To choose the law way is to fall out of or away from the grace way. It is not a case of being in grace and then falling from it. It is a matter of never being in grace. The believer's salvation in the beginning depends not upon what he does but upon what God in Christ has done for him. The permanence of his salvation rests upon the same thing. Man may waver. But Jesus Christ is the same yesterday, today, and forever (Heb. 13:8). See *Grace; Grace, Falling from.*

Sin. The basic Hebrew and Greek words for "sin" both mean "to miss the mark" such as a target. The target is God's character and will. And "all have sinned, and come short of the glory of God" (Rom. 3:23). One may miss the target through bad aim (a false concept of God's righteous nature) or through lack of power to drive a well-aimed arrow to the target (self-effort). Whether one misses the target by an inch or a mile, he misses it. And that constitutes sin. Men weigh sins, but not God. Both murder and false witness are forbidden by the Ten Commandments. Men call one man a murderer and another a liar. God says that both transgressed his will (James 2:10).

The basis of sin is selfishness, centering one's life in his own will rather than in God's will. The greatest of all sins is unbelief as to God's promise to save all who believe in Christ. It is to call God a liar (John 3:16-18). The Christian should avoid sins of the spirit as well as those of the flesh (Col. 3:5,8-9; cf. Matt. 23:13-33). Nowhere has the Bible promised sinless perfection in this life (Rom. 7:14-25; 1 John 1:8 to 2:2).

"The wages of sin is death; but the gift of God is eternal life through Jesus Christ our Lord" (Rom. 6:23; cf. 5:8). See *Perfect; Temptation.*

Soul; Spirit. See *Life.*

Speaking in Tongues. See *Tongues, Speaking in.*

Stewardship. In the New Testament the word "steward" renders two Greek words which are probably synonymous in meaning. One means a person to whom something is committed (Matt. 20:8; Luke 3:3). The other means "house manager" (Luke 16:2). In both cases the person was usually a slave placed over his owner's affairs and other slaves. So "stewardship" means "house management" (Luke 16:2-4).

Unfortunately, "stewardship" is usually limited to money or property. It encompasses all that is placed in one's care by God: self, substance, talents (cf. 1 Cor. 4:1-2; Titus 1:7; 1 Pet. 4:10).

Stumblingblock; Stumblingstone. These words render two Greek words, one meaning something to strike against (Rom. 14:13; 1 Cor. 8:9). At times it is used with "stone" as "a stone of stumbling" (Rom. 9:32-33; 1 Pet. 2:8). The other word is one transliterated into English as "scandal." It refers basically to a trap set for someone to stumble over (Rom. 11:9; Rev. 2:14). However, in 1 Corinthians 1:23 Paul uses it to refer to a crucified Christ as a stumblingblock to Jews. God did not set a trap for them. But their false concept of the Messiah as a political-military figure became a trap they laid for themselves.

Superscription. This renders a Greek word meaning "a writing upon" or "above." In Matthew 22:20 it refers to the designation on a coin. The other use is of a board nailed above Jesus' head on the cross to indicate the reason for his crucifixion (cf. Matt. 27:38; Mark 15:26; Luke 23:38; John 19:19). Note that while the wording varies, one thing is in common: Jesus died as "The King of the Jews."

Temperance. This word renders a family of Greek words meaning mastery or self-control (Acts 24:25; 1 Cor. 9:25; Gal. 5:23; Titus 1:8; 2 Pet. 1:6). These references may be related to any kind of conduct. In Titus 2:2 it translates a word meaning sound-minded or prudent.

Temptation. The Greek word so translated means to test or try as metal to see if it is genuine. In each case the context must decide. For instance, Satan tempts men to prove them false; God tests them to prove them genuine (James 1:13-15).

Jesus was tempted in all points like as men are, yet without sin (Heb. 4:15). For this reason he can help others endure temptation (1 Cor. 10:13; Heb. 4:16). Matthew 4:1 says that Jesus was led by the Spirit into the wilderness "to be tempted" of the devil. This is an infinitive of purpose. So the initiative was with God. Satan tried to prove Jesus false; God would prove him genuine. Jesus' temptations were in three areas: physical appetite (Matt. 4:3); aesthetic nature (do the unusual, Matt. 4:6); ambition (Matt. 4:9). These were the same areas in which Eve was tempted (Gen. 3:6). The devil has no new tricks. But when he fails to snare one in the physical nature he moves into the spiritual one.

Jesus was tempted in his humanity, and he resisted in the same. He succeeded through prayer, Scripture, dedication to God's will, and the power of the Holy Spirit. Every man should do the same. See *Satan; Devil.*

Tongues, Speaking in. The Greek word for "tongue" is *glōssa.* Thus "speaking in tongues" is called "glossolalia" (combining the word for "tongue" with the verb "to speak"). Speaking in tongues is largely treated in Acts 2:1-13 and 1 Corinthians 12–14, especially chapter 14. References to speaking in tongues are also found in Acts 10:44-46; 11:15; 19:6. (Mark 16:17 is not in the best texts, which end with verse 8.) All but Pentecostals generally see this phenomenon at Pentecost (Acts 2) as the ability to speak languages other than one's own without studying them to enable the disciples to preach to those present from throughout the Roman empire (Acts 2:8-11). Some see other like phenomena in Acts as new converts praising God in their own languages. One cannot be dogmatic here.

In 1 Corinthians 12-14 "tongues" or "languages" is a gift of the Holy Spirit given to certain ones (12:10). Some see this as a heavenly language spoken in ecstasy, and thus different from the phenomenon at Pentecost. Whatever it may be, Paul did not place great value on it; in gifts of the Holy Spirit it is last except for "interpretation." In chapter 14 he values "prophecy" or preaching the gospel in plain language above it. In Galatians 5:22-23 he does not list "tongues" as part of the fruit of the Spirit. He certainly did not see this as evidence of spiritual excellence.

The New Testament knows nothing about an *unknown* tongue. Note that this word is in italics in chapter 14, showing that it is not in the Greek text (vv. 2,4,13,19,27). The word "tongues" has taken on a certain theological connotation. If the word "languages" were used it would help to clarify the picture (cf. 14:21). In the writer's opinion every reference to "tongues" in this chapter makes better sense if regarded as languages spoken on earth. Interpreters would be needed to interpret for those present but not familiar with the language spoken.

Thus the writer's personal opinion is that the gift of "tongues" at Pentecost and Corinth are the same. Only at Corinth they were abusing this gift as all others of the Holy Spirit, making them matters of pride and division instead of using them for their intended purpose. As the commercial capital of the empire with its polyglot of people and languages, Corinth would be a logical place for the gift as at Pentecost. Some may have pretended to have the gift who did not, being influenced by the ecstatic utterances of women at the pagan Delphi Oracle and the nearby temple of Aphrodite (cf. 11:5-6; 14:34-35). Paul's primary purpose in dealing with tongues was that it was a major problem in the church. First Corinthians 13:8 says that "tongues . . . shall cease." I see no similarity between modern glossolalia and "tongues" in the New Testament.

The Gospels make no reference to tongues. Jesus never spoke in tongues or promised that his followers would (see above on Mark 16:17b). In his great passage on the Holy Spirit he said nothing about it. It should be noted, however, that many capable, dedicated scholars see otherwise. Each must interpret it as he sees it.

Transfiguration of Jesus. This event took place at night on the lofty slopes of Mount Hermon, eight days after Peter's confession of Jesus as the Christ of God (Luke 9:20,28). The fashion of Jesus' countenance was altered, and his clothing was white and glistening. Moses and Elijah, symbolic of law and prophets (Jewish Scriptures), spoke with Jesus about his "decease" or exodus out of the world (Luke 9:30-31).

Probably Jesus' appearance was his deity shining forth from within. This happened "as he prayed" (v. 29). Evidently he was praying for such a demonstration that his three disciples could see which would convince them of his coming death and resurrection (cf. Matt. 16:21-23). They saw their *Scriptures* teaching the same thing. And they heard God's voice of approval and admonishing them to hear his Son (Matt. 17:5). There is poetic beauty and meaning in the words, "They saw no man, save Jesus only" (Matt. 17:8). Later Peter mentioned this experience (2 Pet. 1:16-18).

Tribulation. The word so translated means to be in a tight place with seemingly no way out, like grapes in the winepress. The verb form is used ten times in the New Testament (Matt. 7:14, "narrow"; Mark 3:9, "throng"; 2 Cor. 1:6; 4:8; 7:5; 1 Thess. 3:14; 2 Thess. 1:6-7; 1 Tim. 5:10; Heb. 11:37). The noun form is used forty-five times, twenty-one as "tribulation" and seventeen as "affliction." Jesus spoke of it as the trials through which his followers would pass in spreading the gospel (John 16:33). He also referred to the "great tribulation" attending the fall of Jerusalem in A.D. 70 (Matt. 24:21). Some see a period of "great tribulation" shortly before the end of the age. However, Matthew 24:21 seems to question this position. Details in eschatology are not a test of orthodoxy. See *Patience*.

Trinity. This word does not appear in the Bible. But it is clear that the one God reveals himself as Father, Son, and Spirit (Matt. 28:19). It is a revealed doctrine, not one arrived at by human reasoning. Yet it submits itself to reason. See *God; Jesus Christ; Holy Spirit*.

True Israel, The. In Exodus 19:1-8 God entered into a covenant of law and works with Israel. It was a conditional one (note "if" and "then," v. 5). Until Israel kept the "if" God was not bound by the "then." History records that as a nation Israel did not honor the "if." Even in the Old Testament the true Israel was the faithful remnant within the nation. Paul recognizes this fact in Romans 9:6. Jeremiah 31:31-34 points to a new covenant which the author of Hebrews sees fulfilled in Christ and his people (8:8 to 10:17). In Matthew 21:33-45 Jesus pictured the faithlessness of Israel, pointing out that "The kingdom of God shall be taken from you, and given to a nation bringing forth the fruits thereof" (v. 43, note also vv. 44-45).

In 1 Peter 2:1-10 the apostle shows that the true Israel today is composed of those who have believed in Jesus as Savior. Note in verses 6-9 how he combines the language of Exodus 19 and Matthew 21. Verse 10 means that this true Israel is not a constituted national entity, but is composed of people out of all national and ethnic groups (see Rev. 5:9-10). So today Christians are the true Israel of God. This is the sense of Romans 11:26.

In Romans 9—11 Paul does picture a time when many Jews will turn to Christ. But they will be saved as individuals, not as a nation, even as Gentiles are saved (Acts 15:11). And all who do believe in Christ as Savior will also be a part of the true Israel. See *Church*.

Truth. Words used to express this idea connote constancy, firmness, faithfulness, and belief. Truth is one of the attributes of God. In a practical sense it is practically equivalent to his revealed will (John 17:17). Jesus said, "I am . . . the truth" (John 14:6). God's ultimate truth is revealed in him (John 8:32,36).

Unbelief. This word translates a Greek word meaning "disobedience" (in Romans 11:30,32; Heb. 4:6,11). Otherwise it renders a word meaning "no faith." But in essence the Greek words express kindred ideas. Because of no faith in God men are disobedient. Unfortunately, "unbelief" is sometimes taken to mean to *unbelieve* (quit believing) something once believed, hence apostasy. A case in point is Hebrews 3:12. The reference is to Israel's rebellion at Kadeshbarnea (Num. 14). Israel did not *unbelieve* her deliverance from Egypt. That was a fact of history. She had *no faith* that God could lead her into Canaan. It was not a renouncing of a past faith; it was a matter of no faith in future events. See *Faith; Grace; Salvation; Security of the Believer.*

Uncleanness. In the New Testament the scribes and Pharisees had brought Old Testament rules about unclean food and ceremonial defilement to apply to men. Thus they kept pots of water handy for ceremonial baths and/or washing the hands or utensils before eating. This is reflected in Matthew 15:3-20; Mark 7:6-23. Such washing had nothing to do with physical but ceremonial cleanliness: lest one's robes had unknowingly brushed against a Gentile or Gentile hands had touched the eating utensils. The washing of hands was even related to the belief that a demon got on the hands and entered the body through the mouth.

Jesus brushed aside all such traditions, showing that man was defiled by what came out of his mouth, not by what went into it (Matt. 15:17-20). Compare "purging all meats" (Mark 7:19) with Peter's vision at Joppa (Acts 10:13-15).

Unpardonable Sin, The. This sin is taught in Matthew 12:22-32 (cf. Mark 3:22-30). Negatively: It is not murder or taking the Lord's name in vain; it is not a sin of ignorance or committed in passionate anger; it is not simply rejecting Jesus until one dies, though such does seal one's fate; it cannot be committed by a Christian who is already pardoned and saved; one who thinks he has committed it has not, for his consciousness of sin is proof that the Holy Spirit is convicting him of such. Positively: It is a sin committed deliberately and in full knowledge of the facts involved; it is a culmination of a series of rejections of Christ; it is a setting of character in which one has lost all sense of moral and spiritual discrimination, where to one good is evil and evil is good; it is a sin that can be committed in the midst of life so that one loses the ability to repent and believe in Jesus. Some hold that it could be committed only while Jesus was on earth. But he is still here in the presence of the Holy Spirit who figures most prominently in this sin. The writer believes that it can be committed today.

Now note the situation. Jesus cast a demon out of a man. The people saw it and asked if it were not evidence that Jesus was "the Son of David," a Messianic title (Matt. 12:23). The Pharisees saw the same thing, but said that Jesus worked by the power of "Beelzebub the prince of devils" or Satan (v. 24). In a series of pictures Jesus showed how wrong they were (vv. 25-30). Then he said that all manner of sin and blasphemy shall be forgiven men, except blasphemy against the Holy Spirit (vv. 31-32). "Blasphemy" means to speak insultingly against someone.

Jesus' good work was obviously of the Holy Spirit. So the people said. But the Pharisees said it was a work of the evil spirit. Note the loss of moral and spiritual discrimination. Following this line, therefore, salvation itself would be an evil work done by the evil spirit. Continued rejection of Christ today is saying the same thing. Finally one comes to the place where he loses all sense of sin. Like Satan in words from John Milton, he says, "Evil, be thou my good!" So crystallized is his attitude of unbelief that he cannot repent and believe in Christ. The person who says he has no sin of which to be forgiven should beware. He is the one who has or is near to committing this sin. The best insurance against taking this fatal, final step is to receive Christ as one's Savior. See *Sin.*

Vainglory. This renders a Greek word meaning "empty glory" or glory which has no substance. It is rendered "pride" in 1 John 2:16. See also Galatians 5:26; Philippians 2:3. Pride may be good or bad. But vain or empty glory is always bad. It is emptiness, nothingness.

Veil of the Temple. This was a finely woven veil whose colors were blue, purple, and scarlet (Exod. 26:31). It separated the Holy of Holies from the Holy Place in the tabernacle or Temple. Through it only the high priest might enter, and that annually on the *Day of Atonement* (which see).

When Jesus died this veil was torn in two *from top to bottom*, not an act of man but of God (Matt. 27:51; Mark 15:38; Luke 23:45). The Jewish Talmud tells of a quaking of the Temple forty years before its destruction or A.D. 30, the year Jesus died. This could explain the event. Hebrews 10:20 says that Jesus, by his death, opened the way for all believers to come to God "through the veil, that is to say, his flesh."

Virgin. In Isaiah 7:14 this word renders *almah*. This was a young woman of marriageable age presumed to be a virgin. Unfortunately much controversy has raged about using such words as "young woman" and footnoting "virgin" (RSV). In Matthew 1:23 it uses the Greek word *parthenos*, virgin. The Septuagint (Greek translation of the Old Testament made by Jewish scholars) uses this word for "virgin" in Isaiah 7:14. In New Testament times Jewish scholars never interpreted this verse in terms of a virgin birth. The New Testament account of Jesus' virgin birth stems from actual history, not simply an adaptation to Old Testament prophecy. See *Virgin Birth*.

Virgin Birth, The. The virgin birth of Jesus is clearly taught in Matthew 1:18-25; Luke 1:26-38. Some question it because of the silence of Mark, John, and Paul (but see John 1:14; Gal. 4:4). Mark begins his Gospel with the public ministry of Jesus. How many times does the Bible need to record something for it to be true? Luke was a physician and historian whose historical accuracy has stood the test of adverse criticism. And "having traced the course of all things accurately from the first" (1:3), he wrote the most beautiful and complete account of the birth (and also the resurrection) of Jesus.

Mary herself was the first to raise a question as to the "how" of a virgin birth (Luke 1:34). The angel's reply is in keeping with *like* begetting *like:* a horse a horse, a man a man, and God God (v. 35). How else could Jesus be the Son of God? Luke 1:37 reads, literally, "For not impossible alongside God any single word." What God says, he can do (see Matt. 1:20-23). See *Miracle*.

Washing of Feet. In Jesus' day a dinner host usually had a slave to rinse dust from the feet of arriving guests (Luke 7:44). In John

13:1-16 Jesus was the host at the Passover meal. In their prideful self-seeking none of the Twelve would have performed so menial a service. So Jesus did it himself. The "example" of verse 15 is just that. Jesus did not command that footwashing become an ordinance of the church as was true of baptism and the Lord's Supper. Certain groups so regard it, but not on a widespread basis. Jesus set an example to show that greatness in God's sight consists not in having the first place at the table. It lies in rendering the lowest of service. Greatness in the kingdom of God is not determined by how many serve one, but how many one serves (Mark 10:36-45).

Wine. While the Old Testament had several words to denote wine or other stronger alcoholic beverages, the New Testament has only one word for "wine" *(oinos)*. In New Testament times wine was often diluted with water. The wine of Sharon, being a lighter wine, was diluted with two parts of water. Other wines, according to the Talmud, used one part wine and three parts water. Diluted wine in small quantities thus was not intoxicating. Such a wine was drunk at meals since water was scarce and often polluted. The injunction against looking on wine when it is "red" (Prov. 23:31) evidently refers to undiluted wine.

Jesus' first miracle or "sign" of his deity was changing water into wine (John 2:1-11). His enemies called him a "winebibber" (Matt. 11:19; Luke 7:34). While obviously biased and exaggerated, this suggests that as was customary Jesus drank the *diluted* wine served at banquets. Paul told Timothy to take a little wine for a stomach ailment and other recurring infirmities (1 Tim. 5:23). Prohibitions of "wine" and "much wine" for bishops and deacons respectively apparently refer to undiluted wine (1 Tim. 3:3,8).

Wine was used as an antiseptic in treating wounds (Luke 10:34). For ulcers Hippocrates prescribed, "Bind with soft wool, and sprinkle with wine and oil." The contents of "the cup," a particular cup (Luke 22:17), at the Lord's Supper is called "the fruit of the vine" (Matt. 26:29; Mark 14:25; Luke 22:18). Whether this was diluted wine or pure grape juice is a matter of judgment. The writer sees it as the latter. As unleavened bread, with no foreign substance, symbolizes Jesus' pure body, so grape juice, not wine (the product of grape juice and bacteria) would best symbolize his pure blood.

The Bible strongly condemns drunkenness (Luke 21:34; Rom. 13:13; 1 Cor. 5:11; 6:10; Gal. 5:21; Eph. 5:18). Certainly the Bible does not condone the modern alcoholic beverage industry. Indeed, in modern society the use of wine in any form should be gauged by Paul's principle regarding eating meat (1 Cor. 8:13).

Witness. This is one of the great words of the Christian faith. The verb and various noun forms appear one hundred and seventy times in the New Testament. In compound form with other words such as "against" (Matt. 27:13), "in" or "through" (Acts 20:23), "with" (Rom. 8:16), "with-upon" (Heb. 2:4), and "false" (Mark 14:57; 1 Cor. 15:15) the word is also used numerous times.

This family of words is found often in the papyri in the sense of legal witnessing in court or signing as witnesses to legal documents. The basic idea in them, therefore, is a legal one—giving firsthand testimony. This same idea is found in the New Testament (Matt. 18:16; 26:65). John 21:24 may well be the seal of approval as truth on the part of the elders in Ephesus as to the authenticity of the Gospel. One requirement for an apostle was that he be able to give firsthand testimony to Jesus' resurrection (Acts 1:22; cf. 1 Cor. 9:1).

The idea of witnessing to personal experience with Christ colors all references to Christian witnessing (Luke 24:48; Acts 1:8). The value of one's testimony is gauged by his character or credibility. So the Christian should *be* a witness as well as *bear* a witness. See *Martyr*.

Women, The Silence of. In dealing with the problem of tongues, Paul told the women of Corinth to "keep silence in the churches" (1 Cor. 14:34). Yet in the same epistle he speaks of women praying and prophesying or preaching (1 Cor. 11:5; cf. Phil. 4:3). "Silence" seems to refer to the problem of tongues which may have been abused more by women. Perhaps they were not so much exercising the gift as uttering meaningless ecstatic sounds, much like the priestesses in the temple of Aphrodite nearby. These women were used in the sex act to worship this sex deity, In certain rituals they uttered ecstatic sounds. Paul forbade Christian women from doing such, lest they be regarded by outsiders as like the priestesses of Aphrodite. It seems to have dealt with a local situation, and is not to be taken generally. See *Speaking in Tongues.*

Wrath of God. While several other words are used for "wrath" in the New Testament, the principal ones are *thumos* and *orgē*. The former expresses a sudden fierce wrath which soon subsides: cf. the furious burning of dry grass or a volcanic eruption. The latter is a more deep-seated wrath which abides. When used of God it means his abiding, universal opposition to evil (Rom. 1:18). It is not an emotion of God, but his moral and spiritual law in operation. The former may be seen in the destruction of Sodom and Gomorrah. The cities were destroyed, but Lot only a little distance away was safe (Gen. 19:17-25). The latter is seen in Matthew 3:7; like a desert or prairie fire it is everywhere.

Perhaps the best way to present these is to list their occurrence in the New Testament. (*Thumos* is found in Luke 4:28; Acts 19:28; Rom. 2:8; 2 Cor. 12:20; Gal. 5:20; Eph. 4:31; Col. 3:8; Heb. 11:27; Rev. 12:12; 14:8,10,19; 15:1,7; 16:1,19; 18:3; 19:15; *orgē* is used in Matt. 3:7; Mark 3:5; Luke 3:7; 21:23; John 3:36; Rom. 1:18; 2:5,8; 3:5; 4:15; 5:9; 9:22; 12:19; 13:4-5; Eph. 2:3; 4:31; 5:6; Col. 3:6,8; 1 Thess. 1:10; 2:16; 5:9; 1 Tim. 2:8; Heb. 3:11; 4:3; James 1:19-20; Rev. 6:16-17; 11:18; 14:10; 16:19; 19;15.) Note that the former appears in Revelation ten times; the latter six times. Generally the former denotes temporal judgments. But in 16:19; 19:15 the two are combined. "Fierceness" renders *thumos;* "wrath" renders *orgē*.

Where can one flee from a prairie fire? Only where the fire has already burned. Where can one flee from the "wrath" *(orgē)* of God? To Calvary where his abiding, universal opposition to evil was poured out on the cross (2 Cor. 5:21). See *Punishment, Everlasting; Retribution; Sin.*

Yahweh. See *Jehovah.*

Yoke-Fellow. This renders a compound Greek word meaning "yoked with." It was used of those united by any bond: marriage, relationship, labor, study, or business. In the New Testament it occurs only in Philippians 4:3. It evidently refers to someone who formerly had labored with Paul in the gospel in Philippi (Luke, Lydia, Epaphroditus?). The Frenchman Renan suggested that it refers to Lydia who was married to Paul! But the masculine form of "true" rules out this wild speculation.

Some see this as a proper name (Synzygos, Greek, *sunzugos*). Coming in the midst of proper names, this is possible.

Zacharias. This name is important in Christian doctrine only because of Jesus' use of it in Matthew 23:35. He was probably Zechariah the son of Jehoiada (2 Chron. 24:20-22) who was stoned "in the court of the house of the Lord." "Barachias" may mean that Jehoiada was also known by this name.

The point of Jesus' remark is seen in the fact that in the Hebrew canon of Scripture Genesis comes first and 2 Chronicles last. Abel's death is mentioned in the former; Zacharias' death is in the latter. So Jesus was saying that all the blood of martyrs slain and recorded in the Hebrew Scriptures would be required of the Jewish nation in that generation (Matt. 23:36-38). This happened in A.D. 70.

Zion. This name was applied to Jerusalem or certain areas of it since David's time. The name itself is of uncertain meaning, though it probably is related to the Hebrew verb "to protect." Its Arabic equivalent means "ridge of a mountain" or "citadel."

The exact location of the original Zion is a subject of debate. But modern archaeological excavations seem to confirm the position that it was located on the hill Ophel, the southeastern ridge near the Virgin's Fountain. The first mention of Zion is in 2 Samuel 5:7. David took the stronghold of Zion, and it came to be known as the city of David. In the time of the prophets "Zion" was extended to include the Temple area (Isa. 4:5; 8:18; Jer. 31:6; Micah 4:7).

In Christian thought the name apparently referred to the entire city of Jerusalem (Matt. 21:5; John 12:15). In a figurative sense it is used as symbolic of all the people of God (Rom. 9:33; 11:26; 1 Pet. 2:6). Hebrews 12:22 speaks of "Sion" (Greek form) as "the city of the living God, the heavenly Jerusalem" (see verses 22b-24; also Rev. 14:1).